T0090842

UNDERSTANDING THE NATAL CHART

An Esoteric Approach to Learning Horoscopy

Suzanne Rough

authorHOUSE®

AuthorHouse™ UK Ltd.
1663 Liberty Drive
Bloomington, IN 47403 USA
www.authorhouse.co.uk
Phone: 0800.197.4150

© 2014 Suzanne Rough. All rights reserved.

No part of this book may be reproduced, stored in a retrieval system, or transmitted
by any means without the written permission of the author.

Published by AuthorHouse 07/29/2014

ISBN: 978-1-4969-8585-9 (sc)
ISBN: 978-1-4969-8584-2 (e)

Library of Congress Control Number: 2014912409

Any people depicted in stock imagery provided by Thinkstock are models,
and such images are being used for illustrative purposes only.
Certain stock imagery © Thinkstock.

This book is printed on acid-free paper.

Because of the dynamic nature of the Internet, any web addresses or links contained in this book may have changed
since publication and may no longer be valid. The views expressed in this work are solely those of the author and do
not necessarily reflect the views of the publisher, and the publisher hereby disclaims any responsibility for them.

Other Astrological Works by Suzanne Rough

Transitional Astrology: Giving an Esoteric Role to Orthodox Astrology
Working with Time: Understanding and Identifying Opportunity
Understanding Relationship: Synastry and Compository

Contents

Preface

When this work was conceived in the early 2000s, it was with an accompanying chart construction manual, which is not included in this edition. Most people who are interested in astrology have computer-generated charts, either from their own software or astrology websites. Nowadays, this kind of chart is likely to be more reliable than those resulting from a beginner's early, unassisted effort at manual chart construction and has the merit of allowing the student to engage with the kind of ideas that keep interest in the subject alive.

Eventually, all serious students of astrology should learn to manually construct charts, because it shows respect for the discipline and frees them from the restriction imposed by software standardisation, but this can take place at a later stage.

Other changes made for the purposes of this edition are the removal of observations that, twelve years later, no longer have the same relevance.

It is the aim of this revised work to provide that kind of encouragement by indicating the value of the natal chart to the spiritual seeker if it is read in a certain way. It offers guidance in the matter of working with these concepts, regardless of experience levels.

Those who find the ideas in this work interesting and useful are advised to move on to *Transitional Astrology: Giving an Esoteric Role to Orthodox Astrology*, where they are placed in the cosmic context.

Suzanne Rough
April 2014

Introduction

This work is designed to take the committed student of astrology from the very basics of the discipline of horoscopy through to chart readings.

However, any manual can provide only a structure for learning. The learning itself comes from practice.

To get a firm grip on principles, it is important to make astrological knowledge part of everyday life by having an ephemeris on hand in order to know in which sign the Sun, Moon, and the planets are to be found.

As part of the process of tidying away the day, serious students will recapitulate upon all that they have experienced inwardly and outwardly during the course of each day, check out what has been going on in the heavens, and gauge how this has impacted upon their personal energy fields as delineated in a natal chart.

Later, they will examine the lives of those around them using their natal charts.

The intuition will never flow until a personal connection has been made with the body of knowledge we call astrology, and until the intuition flows, the connections required for interpretation will not readily form. As we practice it in the West, astrology is not a science; it is branch of knowledge that confers insight by creating the conceptual conduits and categories through which a higher level of consciousness from that used in everyday life can flow, organise itself, and become accessible to the intellect.

When astrology is practiced as a science, it is mechanistic, dead, and deterministic, and its effect on others is rarely positive. This is not the same thing as saying astrology does not have a need for standards and disciplines: The quality of the conduits created through the application of astrological knowledge will determine the quality of the involvement of that higher level of consciousness, but it is to emphasise the importance of becoming personally involved in the practice of astrology.

Max Weber, the German sociologist, famously posited that it was possible for an anarchist to be a lawyer (i.e. that our private selves and our public functions can operate quite independently of each other). This may indeed be the case, but no students of Western astrology, who are not themselves interested and involved in the development of human consciousness, will make insightful astrologers. Insight comes from living the knowledge.

Part One

Horoscopy's Context

Chapter 1

Astrology in the West

"How can you believe that some lumps of rock whirling around in space can influence us?" a man once said to me in disgust, in the days before I had learned that astrology is best not discussed at social gatherings. I realised then how little respect there is among the general public for both astrologers and their discipline. And why is this? Because so few practitioners themselves understand how and why their discipline works. In the past twenty or so years, interest in astrology may have increased significantly, but can the same be said for either professional standards or public respect? For as long as there is a credibility gap, it falls to astrologers themselves to close it.

***

In the West, the world of astrology is represented by horoscopy or natal astrology. For most Westerners, astrology is horoscopy, a fact that reveals the importance we give to the individual and his psyche but also conceals the richness of the astrological legacy, fed by many different cultures, times, and traditions, that has come down to the modem world.

Although it is so obviously reductive to confine experience of astrology to just one expression, the West has found its relationship with astrology through horoscopy and remains largely unaware and interested in its other branches. That is as it is, and what this focus has brought to horoscopy is a wealth of psychological understanding that has enhanced the practice and value of horoscopy. In the West, astrology has both gained and lost.

From its earliest times, astrology has been a dialogue between man and the heavens. Man has sought to explain occurrences on our planet with reference to what is happening in the heavens. Astrology is essentially a system of explanation. Correspondences were observed between occurrences on Earth and movements in the heavens, assumptions and associations were made, and concepts were created and fed by use. In the presentation of these concepts, causal relationships replaced that of correspondence, and astrology as we understand it today came into being.

Astrology is a dialogue of man with himself about his experience of being in incarnation. It is a dialogue that enables individual men to benefit from the thinking of the collectivity. The zodiac is a repository of human observation and experience.

This knowledge can lock us into the past as does the astrology of those cultures dominated by the idea of fate: It has been this way, it is this way, and it can be no other way, or it can inspire us to access our potential, which is the intention of esoterically oriented astrology. Everything is in a state of becoming.

Through astrology, Western man is dialoguing with himself about his individuality, because it is this that is central to our reality. We experience ourselves as factors of isolated significance who seem to have control over certain things but not others who tend to suffer a great deal. Pain alerts us to the fact that something is wrong. Could the fault just be in us and in the way we deal with life? The assumption is that it must be; otherwise, there would be no expectation that anything could be improved. It is to find out how things might be improved that contemporary Westerners turn to astrology, and our natal astrology is helping to us understand this situation by encouraging us to see that the world we experience is of our own making.

In other parts of the world, people consult astrologers to inquire how many cows will make up a future wife's dowry and how many sons she will bear, but in the West, these are no longer matters that are considered crucial to the way we plan our lives.

Western astrology is evolving in response to the answers raised by perplexed, questing individuals, and as long as someone has some answers to these questions, that can be communicated through the language of astrology, we stand to make some headway.

Trends in Western Astrology

During the course of the twentieth century, Western astrology began to move from the idea of predeterminism toward that of using the natal chart as a guide to using time and energy wisely. With this shift came a realisation that if astrology could be used as a guide in the matter of bringing about desirable change, it could be used in support of spiritual development. It was assumed that if we better understood our energy patterns, we would be able to manage them better and stand a better chance of achieving our spiritual goals. The goals did not come from the body of knowledge that we call astrology but were provided by religious and spiritual thinking. Astrology was merely in the service of them.

Before the Second World War, this development did not involve much more than releasing astrology from the gloom and fear engendered by predeterminism and by encouraging people to live intelligently and accept what they could not change as the will of God.

Charles Carter, then president of the Astrological Lodge and the first principal of the Astrological Lodge, concluded his *Principles of Astrology* (first published in 1925) with the following words:

"For when man sees in all that happens to him or to others the irresistible tide of Providence, willing and accomplishing the highest good of all beings, he then consciously and gladly unites his will to the Divine Will."

Fifty years later, however, in a Western world restored to peace, prosperity, and confidence, changed expectation was giving rise to a new kind of astrology that assumed that if we could only come to understand ourselves better, we could release ourselves from the hold of those influences that limited us and caused us to suffer. Nothing then could hold us back from being what we wanted to be. Rather than laying out how things would be, the natal chart became viewed as the guide to realising potential and fulfilment.

It was during the 1970s that spirituality, perhaps under the influence of the drug culture, began to depart company with effort and became focused on attainment and altering consciousness: on arriving rather than journeying.

By the 1980s, astrology was joining hands with psychology and the journeying that was done was into the psyche. Some very good work was done in these years that raised the profile of astrology, but when it became apparent that psychology was also simply a system of explanation and had no answers to give, it was only a matter of time before psychologically oriented astrology would fail to satisfy. Excellent in the service of explaining why things were as they were, neither psychology nor psychological astrology could help people understand what was the purpose of being here or where to move onto.

There was a time when self-knowledge was thought to be that purpose, but by the close of the twentieth century, it became apparent that that too was only a step on the way.

Esoteric Astrology

At the start of the twenty-first century, the demand is increasingly for esoteric astrology. But what is this esoteric astrology? The fact is that few really know, and most, when they turn to Alice Bailey's *Esoteric Astrology* (Endnote 1) for illumination, cannot see what this work has to do with astrology at all because it is not concerned with the individual or natal astrology.

Esoteric astrology, properly defined, is the astrology of the soul. It is not person-centred, and it is not at all what most people want when they are still in personality consciousness and suffering and unfulfilled because of it. It is not the soul that causes us problems, but rather the layers of personality consciousness that impede soul expression.

Far more practically useful for the people we are is conventional person-centred astrology with an esoteric orientation that uses the natal chart as a way to acquire understanding about ourselves and how to engage with the world. Purpose (understanding it and living it out) is now a potent spiritual idea and the key to soul-personality alignment.

Again, this key has not come from astrology; it has come from where answers and keys have ever come, and that is from the spiritual plane, through the agency of our spiritual teachers, philosophers, and poets. Astrology itself cannot give answers. It deals in explanations. That is something different. Astrology, however, may be able to incorporate those explanations and help them enter consciousness. It is a system of explanation that can be made to disclose much. But it is important to understand that astrology itself says nothing, and astrological charts do not speak any more than a flute that is not blown can play music. They are both instruments, they both need operatives, and they are both man made.

So, coming back to natal charts, if they are to help us understand how to live better and develop potential, then they have to be read in a certain way, working from certain assumptions with a certain understanding and observing certain disciplines. And it is this process that we are embarking upon in this work.

The Natal Chart as a Map

Some definitions:

Ecliptic	The path that, to the observer on Earth, the Sun appears to travel as it orbits Earth. In reality, of course, it is Earth transiting the Sun.
Plane	Level
Great circle	Any circle, the plane of which passes through the centre of Earth. The three great circles of horizon, equator, and ecliptic are the main circles of reference for locating any planet's position relative to any place on Earth, although reference must be made also to the prime vertical, which is a determinant of the vernal point.

Vernal point	Point of interception of the equator and the prime vertical
Luminaries	The Sun and the Moon
Hylegs	A rather old-fashioned term that is nevertheless useful to describe the places of interception between great circles and the ecliptic which give the astrologer four of the most important points in any natal chart: the ascendant, descendant, MC (midheaven - Medium Coell), and the IC (Imam Coeli).

To be strictly correct, when talking about the physical properties of the luminaries, one should use the lowercase, as do scientists and laypeople. The Sun and Moon (uppercase) describe the symbols belonging to astrology. In practice, it is too complicated to switch and change between the two, so in this book, we use only the uppercase versions.

About the natal chart document

- The natal chart is still of the heavens at the moment when the baby established independent breathing. For the astrologer, this, not the physical appearance, is the moment of birth.
- The natal chart is a view of the heavens from the place on Earth where the birth occurred.
- The natal chart is a two-dimensional calibration of a moment in time in our three-dimensional world. The loss of a dimension creates certain distortions, but this is not the concern of the astrologer who studies what the map shows. Astrology itself is constructed around the illusion that the Sun moves around Earth, describing as it does so the circle we call the ecliptic. The patterns in the heavens as seen from the place of birth imprints the subtle bodies of the baby as he is born, to create an inner sky or blueprint.

Figure 1 The three-dimensional representation.
Figure 2 The situation from the point of view of the observer at the place of birth.
Figure 3 The situation in Figure 2 displayed as a natal chart in what has become the standard Western format.

Figure 1

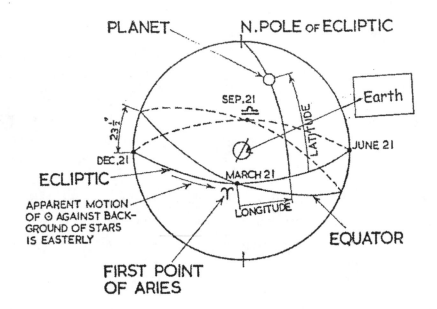

Figure 2

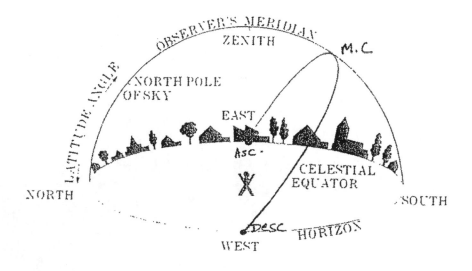

Figure 3

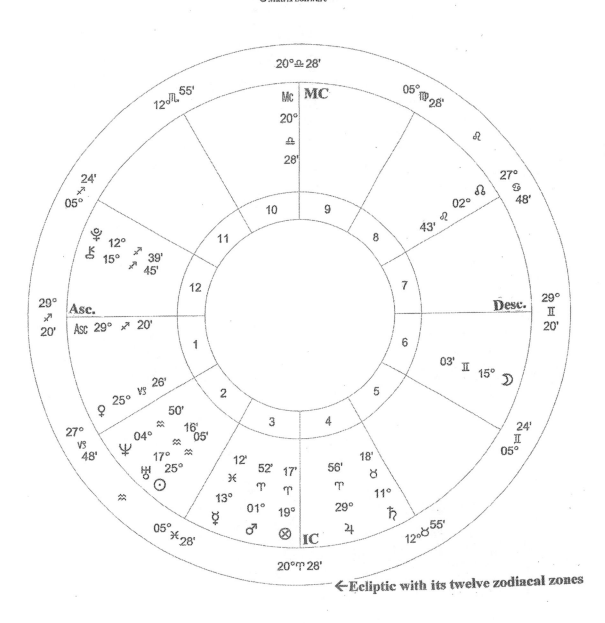

Valentine (male)
February 14th 2000
San Fransisco; CA; USA
03:50 PST
Koch House system
© Matrix Software

←**Ecliptic with its twelve zodiacal zones**

There are only a few more points to be made at this stage:

- The top of the chart is the view looking south, not north, as would be the case with a terrestrial map. This means that the ascendant, which is the easterly point of interception, is on the left of the chart. The opposite point of interception in the west is the descendant. These points form two of the four hyleg points.
- The MC in the south is the most elevated point of the chart, but please note that this is not directly overhead (see Figure 2 for clarification). The opposite point in the north is the IC. These are the remaining two hyleg points.

The planets are in the chart, by means of coordinates, just as one would locate a place in a terrestrial map. Astrology uses celestial longitude, which belongs to the ecliptic system, and declination, which belongs to the equatorial system. We will deal with this in Part Two.

Endnote

1. *Esoteric Astrology*, The Lucis Trust, published in 1951.

Chapter 2

An Esoteric View of the Universe

If you have never met with such ideas before, much of what is contained in this section may seem bizarre and even disturbing. Generally speaking, people who are interested in spirituality have no awareness of the context or understanding of the purpose served by spirituality. They are focused upon what they must try to do to live better. This is adequate for practical, everyday purposes, but lack of a context is one of the biggest causes of distortion in contemporary spiritual thinking and by (knock-on effect) upon our expectations. An astrologer whose basic tools are systemic energies must have an awareness of context, and this means of our solar system.

*** *** ***

The student of esotericism comes to understand that the universe is because of life, quality, and appearance: Everything in manifestation is the result of the coming together of these three forces.

- Life is the first principle.
- Quality or consciousness is the second principle.
- Appearance or fusion is the third principle.

These three interact constantly (imagine a moving triangle), and the third principle, appearance, or fusion, which is expressive of both life and quality, can become the first principle in a similar triadal relationship on a lower level.

An esotericist needs to be able to identify the first, second, and third principles in any manifestation.

The serious student of astrology needs to understand, at the very least, that the universe is a vast system of give and take.

- Life (first principle) is given by a higher level to a lower level that manifests for this purpose.
- Appearance (third principle).
- The lower level then processes the energy of life and returns it in the form of quality (consciousness: second principle).

- The energy of consciousness is them passed back to the level of appearance for it to pass on, as the first principle of a lower triad.

The downward flow is involutionary and is concerned with the creation of lower levels: The energy that is returned is evolutionary and is concerned with freeing itself from form.

The downward flow has created the ray of creation:

Absolute
All starry worlds
Constellation and Suns of the Milky Way
-- *into our solar system*
Sun
planets
organic life *on* Earth, *including humanity*
***into* the body of Earth**
Moon

The flow of force down the ray of creation is as follows:

- The absolute distributes energy to the constellations of the Milky Way, which processes it and then sends it back in the form of consciousness to the starry worlds.
- The starry worlds then send it back to the constellations, which send it down to the planets of our solar system.
- The planets receive energy from outside our solar system, from the constellations and return processed energy in the form of consciousness to the Sun .
- The Sun gives that energy back to the planets.
- The planets give our energy to organic life living on the surface of Earth.
- Organic life on Earth processes it and releases it at death to the Moon or sends it back during the lifetime to the planets in the form of consciousness. This is the first time that an option enters into distribution arrangements, and that option is made available through humanity.

Distribution of energy in our solar system (involutionary):

Constellations of the Milky Way
Sun
Planets
Organic life on Earth, *including unconscious humanity*
Earth
Moon

The human kingdom is the variable factor in nature's distribution arrangements. If a man is conscious and lives consciously, the energy he generates will be of a high enough quality to be returned to the planets. If he does not refine his energy then, at death with that of the other kingdoms of nature, it will go to the Moon to extend the involutionary ray of creation. In time, our Moon will develop its own Moon.

Raising the level of the energy that we transform while in incarnation is the basic purpose being served by our spiritual and religious systems that encourage us to live consciously.

Distribution of energy in our solar system with a conscious participation from the human kingdom (evolutionary):

Constellations of the Milky Way

Sun

Planets

Organic life on Earth

Conscious humanity

planets

Within the universe, participation from the human kingdom creates a third evolutionary triad. The next triad created by organic life, the Moon, and the body of the Earth remains involutionary, something of which the esoterically oriented astrologer needs to be aware when trying to understand the significance of the Moon. We will deal with this later in the course.

	Life 1	**Quality 2**	**Appearance 3**
Triad one	Absolute	All starry worlds	Constellations of the Milky Way
Triad two	Constellations of the Milky way	Our Sun	Planets of our solar system
Triad three	Planets of our solar system	Conscious members of the human kingdom	Organic life on earth: human, animal, vegetable, a n d mineral kingdoms

Western astrology is concerned with the third triad, which contains conscious humanity. It deals with:

- The down-flowing of energy from the Sun via the planets (first principle)
- The humans in incarnation who, with the other kingdoms of nature, are receptors of this energy (third principle)
- The conscious human's experience and understanding of what to do with this energy (second principle)

This third triad is constantly moving: Consciousness of the experience of receiving energy may bring about changes in the way that energy is received and thereby change an individual's quality of being. Changes in quality of being may, in turn, influence the kind and amount of energy an individual can receive. In this situation, the power of the human mind is very influential, and astrology, which records and facilitates this exchange, can serve the purpose of raising quality of being and thereby the vibration of the energy generated.

The natal chart shows:

- How an individual receives from the higher levels (i.e. it shows him as a receptor)
- How he will experience the donation of planetary energy
- How he can use it most efficiently
- Where the energy flow will be blocked and frustrated giving rise to problems and ill health

Natal astrology enables us to read and understand the energy pattern of each human being. To this, we can apply our knowledge of the rate of orbital motions and habits of the planets and are able to anticipate the kind of influences an individual will be coming under and how this is likely to be experienced. This knowledge makes possible prediction, including the identification of opportunities.

The Theosophical Tradition

With Madame Blavatsy and theosophy, esoteric thinking in the West came to focus upon the consciousness within the form and not upon the form itself. In consequence, the Bailey books use different terms of reference from those used in this lesson so far. But it does not take much to bring them into alignment.

Theosophy talks about seven levels of consciousness on seven planes of nature. Students who are familiar with the Bailey books may be able to deduce that:

- Triad one represents the cosmic mental plane.
- Triad two represents the cosmic astral plane
- Triad three represents the cosmic physical plane
- Studying the table below reminds us that:
- The Sun and the planets are the phenomenal appearance of beings with their own emotional and spiritual natures and the stars are the phenomenal appearance of beings with a spiritual nature. All have purposes unknown to man, who must concern himself with his own purpose.
- The higher is contained in the lower and that in our own mental and astral bodies (see next section), we contain a reflection of the cosmic mental and astral planes. We ourselves are a universe in miniature.

Ray of creation - evolving levels	Cosmic physical plane	Physical plane	Representing cosmic astral plane	Representing cosmic mental plane
Absolute	◆			◆
all starry worlds	◆			◆
constellations and Suns of the Milky Way	◆			◆
our Sun	◆		◆	
planets	◆		◆	
Life on Earth collectively	◆	◆		
individual units of life on Earth, *including conscious humanity*	◆	◆		

The Human Being as a Receptor of Energy

The human being receives energy from the Sun and planets through his etheric body. In astrology, the etheric body is often called the sidereal body. The word sidereal comes from the Latin sidus, which means star.

So what and where is the sidereal body?

The idea of the higher being contained within the lower is central to esoteric thinking. Thus, it is, as we saw in the previous section, that the cosmic mental plane is contained within the cosmic astral plane, and both the cosmic mental plane and the cosmic astral plane are contained within the cosmic physical plane (triads one, two, and three); thus, it is that the Absolute is contained within each individual unit of life on Earth. These ideas are usually too much for a student just beginning to engage with an esoteric discipline, but it may be becoming apparent why it is so difficult for science and esotericism to find common ground: Science starts from the dense physical, which for the esotericist is the lowest possible level, and esotericism starts from a level which for the scientist does not exist. The scientist sees lumps of rocks whirling in space, while the esotericist understands that they are the physical manifestation of a higher reality.

The etheric or sidereal body is a higher body that interpenetrates the lower, dense physical body. People with etheric vision can see it in the form of an egg-shaped aura. It is the transmitting station for the human being. This is where solar and planetary energies register, and it is this that the natal chart depicts.

There are seven major (plus a far greater number of less significant) reception centres in the etheric body. They are called chakras, a term the West has taken from the East.

The higher chakras are those positioned in the body above the diaphragm. Opening these chakras is the purpose of spiritual awareness. The chakras below the diaphragm are open in all human beings.

The chakras are an area of study in their own right, and we are not attempting to deal with them in any detailed way in this course, but it is important for the student of astrology to understand that the natal chart depicts the etheric body, the place where solar and planetary energies enter the body.

As you will see in Part Two where we study the houses, the etheric body in itself contains yet higher bodies in the form of the intellectual, astral (emotional), and mental (spiritual) bodies.

The dense physical body (i.e. our flesh and bones) clothes the etheric vehicle.

In esoteric thinking, the etheric body is the physical body, the dense physical body being nothing but the outer expression of this. Anything that manifests in the dense physical body has its cause in a higher body.

The implications of this for our understanding of illness and healing are enormous, but that too is a separate area of study. That study has to take into account not simply the fact that, in the opinion of most people, astrology is not considered sufficiently authoritative to be dealing with the matter of illness, but also the reasons why we humans hold onto ill health. It is a buffer against many things, including change.

The constitution of a human being:

level of consciousness	vehicle	chakra	Correspondence
Soul:	spiritual soul	crown	Absolute
	ego	ajna	all starry worlds
---------------------	---------------------	---------------------	
Personality:	mental	throat	constellations and Suns of the Milky Way
	higher astral	heart	Sun
	---------------------astral	---------------------	
		solar plexus	planets
	etheric		
	---------------------dense	sacral	life on Earth
	physical	---------------------	
		base	individual unit

14

The process we call spirituality is an ongoing and objective process, involving the opening the seven major energy centres, and serving the requirements of the system in which we take our place. By this means, with the

opening of each chakra, we access another level of consciousness. With the higher chakras open, we can return processed energy to the planets that brought it to us and help them to make their return to the Sun .

The spiritual journey may bring different people different kinds of experience, but we are all travelling the same road, and the fuel for the journey is the same: It comes from transforming lower energy into higher.

In this task of transforming energy, the natal chart, which is essentially a chart of our energy field and a map of the four subtle bodies of the personality, can be an invaluable guide. Used in this way, we shift the focus of astrology from being a study of what influences are raining down on us from above to a study of how best we can transform energy and make our return.

To summarise:

- The planets receive energy from outside our solar system from the constellations and return processed energy to the Sun .
- The Sun gives that energy back to the planets.
- The planets give energy to organic life living on the surface of our planet, which includes the human family.
- Organic life on Earth sends the energy on to the Moon, although from the more conscious of the human family with chakras above the diaphragm open, a return may be made to the planets by letting them express their quality through us. This is the path of return, which is the concern of every spiritual tradition.

Chapter 3

Introducing the Zodiac

The language of astrology is becoming increasingly familiar, and for that reason, the function of the teacher, be that a person or a work of instruction, is changing. It is no longer necessary to have to spend a lot of/ time describing the qualities of the signs and the planets. This kind of information is widely available now, and most people who are interested in astrology will have already picked up quite a lot of sound, basic information from mass-market books before embarking upon any formal study. The teacher's task is to encourage a way of thinking that will enable people to gain a better understanding of the esoteric setting in which astrology has its place and the evolutionary process that it serves. We will call this astrology's context. Take the elements, for example, there are probably few people interested in astrology who do not know to which element is ascribed each a/ the signs, even if they may need reminding that Aquarius is an air and not a water sign. What is needed is an understanding of what the elements represent. It is through raising the level of explanation that we will help to raise the standard of astrological practice.

✳✳✳

Astrological tradition recognises two zodiacs: the sidereal and the tropical. Both are man-made constructs that overlay the constellations bearing the same names, which are found close to the celestial equator. Both comprise the same twelve signs, each comprising thirty degrees and both begin with the first point of Aries (Aries 0 degrees).

The sidereal zodiac is more closely aligned with the constellations and is used in Eastern astrology. Western astrology has come to favour the tropical zodiac, which makes the point of interception between the prime vertical and the equator, also known as the vernal point, the start of the zodiac (or Aries 0 degrees). This is a moving point because of a process called the precession of the equinoxes, so the signs of the Western tropical zodiac are moved out of alignment with the constellations that give them their names.

At present, Aries 0 degrees (the vernal point), is against the backdrop of the constellation Pisces, retrograding toward the constellation Aquarius.

Over the course of 26,000 years, the vernal point moves backward through all the constellations spending approximately 2,100 years in each sign. Only when the vernal point has moved back against the constellation Aries will the signs of the Western zodiac be aligned once more with the constellations of the same name. We are not expecting this to occur for another 22,000 years, unless the Earth shifts on its axis.

This regression of the vernal point gives us the Great Year and also changes the pole star, but this is rather more detail that we need to go into here.

The sidereal zodiac does not move in this way, and the difference between the two now is approximately twenty-five degrees and getting wider. The moving zodiac retains its inner structure, however, and features all twelve signs, each of thirty degrees and always in the same order.

Why the West has adopted the moving zodiac rather than the sidereal zodiac is an interesting matter and one that is beyond the scope of this course. Our concern is to offer a way of thinking about the signs that comprise it. Firstly, what is the purpose of this man-made construct that compacts the sprawling constellations into tidy even zones of thirty degrees each and borrows their names?

According to Master DK, the zodiac came into being in the Atlantean era, a mental construct with a job to do. That job was to reflect stellar energy and make it able to enter human consciousness. As you may remember from Chapter Two, energy from the constellations enters our solar system by means of the planets, which then send the energy to the Sun, which processes it and sends it back to the planets. The planets then pass the energy down to organic life on Earth. This is part of the down-flow that is life.

The signs of the zodiac describe, in terms that are intelligible to humanity, the quality of energy transmitted by the constellations of the same name. But does the fact that the signs of the tropical zodiac are out of alignment with the constellations that they are representing mean the energy of each sign is less pure than it was in the days when it was aligned? This has to remain a theoretical proposition. The fact is that the movement is so slow that we cannot hope to know this by empirical methods of research.

The zodiac is part of the process of getting that energy *back* from humanity in the form of consciousness. The zodiac helps man understand the quality of the energy that is working on him and helps him to work with it. The more conscious he is of it, the more it conditions him and influences his experience of planetary energies (remember the moving triangle: life, quality, and appearance).

As each luminary and planet moves through the zodiac (i.e. around the ecliptic), it retains its essential nature but takes on the influence of the sign or zone of influence. Venus, for example, is always Venus, but one does not have to work with astrology for long to recognise that the energy that comes from Venus in Scorpio is very different from that which comes from Venus in Pisces.

The zodiac, therefore, assists the process of coming to consciousness.

Secondly, each sign of the Zodiac comprises three decanates (ten degrees), and by a process called correspondence, or the same principle working on a different level:

- The first decanate incorporates the first principle, life.
- The second incorporates the second principle, quality or consciousness.
- The third decanate incorporates the third principle, appearance or fusion.
- We will look at what this means when we look at each of the signs of the zodiac. To summarise:
- The constellations of the Milky Way send their energy to the planets which then process it and return it to the Sun .
- This level of exchange is of too high a vibration for man to engage with and so the construction that is the zodiac offers to man a reflection of this process.
- The zodiacal signs or zones of influence condition the behaviour of the luminaries and the planets when they appear to move into them.
- The purpose of the zodiac is to help man better understand the planetary energies that are influencing him and enable him to use them more constructively.

The Signs of the Zodiac

The Signs and their Glyphs

It may be a little pedantic to talk about glyphs and not symbols, but one of the difficulties that a student frequently runs into is confusing signs and planets. So it is advisable to keep them apart from the outset by talking about zodiacal glyphs and planetary symbols.

Zodiacal sign	Representing Zodiacal degrees	Glyph	Masculine (M) / feminine (F)
Aries	0-29	♈	M
Taurus	30-59	♉	F
Gemini	60-89	♊	M
Cancer	90-129	♋	F
Leo	130-159	♌	M
Virgo	160-189	♍	F
Libra	190-219	♎	M
Scorpio	220-249	♏	F
Sagittarius	250-279	♐	M
Capricorn	280-299	♑	F
Aquarius	300-329	♒	M
Pisces	330-359	♓	F

Conventional astrology recognises three major ways of classifying the signs:

1. Polarities based on the duality of self/other (which is a lower correspondence of the personality/soul duality) describes the focus of the sign.

self-aware	other-aware	polarity expressed in glyphs
Aries	Libra	♈------------♎
Taurus	Scorpio	♉------------♏
Gemini	Sagittarius	♊------------♐
Cancer	Capricorn	♋------------♑
Leo	Aquarius	♌------------♒
Virgo	Pisces	♍------------♓

2.   Triplicities based on element - describes the nature of the sign

Fire	Water	Air	Earth
Aries	Cancer	Gemini	Taurus
Leo	Scorpio	Libra	Virgo
Sagittarius	Pisces	Aquarius	Capricorn

The elements are the physical plane expression of:

*   Fire: spirit (the quality of the mental plane)
*   Water: emotion (the quality of the astral plane)
*   Air: intellect (the quality of the etheric plane)
*   Earth: materiality (the quality of physical plane itself)

3.   Quadruplicities based on quality - describes the mode of the sign

Cardinal	Mutable	Fixed
Aries	Gemini	Taurus
Cancer	Virgo	Leo
Libra	Sagittarius	Scorpio
Capricorn	Pisces	Aquarius

* The quadruplicities are often referred to as the qualities.

*   The cardinal signs are initiating
*   The mutable signs are experimenting
*   The fixed signs are perservering

Using these guidelines, we can begin to build a picture of each of the signs

Sign	Glyph	Focus	Nature	Mode
Aries	♈	self/personality	spirited	initiating
Taurus	♉	self/personality	material	persevering
Gemini	♊	self/personality	intellectual	experimenting
Cancer	♋	self/personality	emotional	initiating
Leo	♌	self/personality	spirited	persevering
Virgo	♍	self/personality	material	experimenting
Libra	♎	other/soul	intellectual	initiating
Scorpio	♏	other/soul	emotional	perserving
Sagittarius	♐	other/soul	spirited	experimenting
Capricorn	♑	other/soul	material	initiating
Aquarius	♒	other/soul	intellectual	perserving
Pisces	♓	other/soul	emotional	experimenting

It is good practice to write out the glyphs out until they can be remembered effortlessly, as well as the polarities, because this knowledge is needed in chart construction, The triplicities and the quadruplicities are significant in chart interpretation.

Chapter 4

Zodiacal Profiles

Read anything you can find on the signs of the zodiac, from popular astrology to Alice Bailey. It will all help build a working knowledge. The aim of these profiles is to draw attention to the most important characteristics of each sign.

***

Aries - The Ram

♈

A polarity with Libra
Element: Fire (spirited)
Mode: Cardinal (initiating)

- Experience brought to the personality : assertiveness
- Contribution made through this sign: vitality and new beginnings

The energy of Aries is:

- Initiating: Starts things but finds it difficult to see them through once routine replaces creativity
- Original: Sees a value in something before it is commonly accepted
- Spontaneous: Likes things to happen straight away and loses interest if there is any delay
- Energetic: Pulls out all the stops and goes for it
- Liberating: Releases energy trapped in stagnant situations on the mental, emotional, or physical level
- Focused: Not easily distracted from within by self-doubt and second thoughts, nor from without by the reactions of others
- Forgiving: Moves on quickly from personal hurts and loses interest in grievances

- Selfish: Aware of and interested only in its own reality and interests
- Restless: Mentally, emotionally and physically

The key to understanding the expression of Aries is the need to break new ground constantly

Of Aries, *Esoteric Astrology* says:

- "And the Word said: Let form again be sought." *(Ordinary man)*
- "I come forth and from the plane of mind I rule." *(Developed man)*

Taurus: The Bull

♉

A polarity with Scorpio
Element : Earth (material)
Mode: Fixed (persevering)

- Experience brought to the personality: acquisitiveness
- Contribution made through this sign : stability

The energy of Taurus is:

- Steadfast: Unlikely to encourage second thoughts and changes of mind
- Grounded: Building from the foundations upward
- Consolidating: Liking security and stability
- Determined: Finding merit in sticking at things rather than moving on
- Patient: Unconcerned with how long things take to happen
- Pacific: Dislikes disharmony and destructiveness
- Sensuous: Likes things that appeal to the five senses
- Conservative: Disinclined to take risks
- Stubborn: Not willing to move on

The key to understanding the expression of Taurus is that it strives to consolidate.

Of Taurus, *Esoteric Astrology* says:

- "And the Word said: Let struggle be undismayed." *(Ordinary man)*
- "I see and when the Eye is open all is light." *(Developed man)*

Gemini: The Twins

♊

A polarity with Sagittarius
Element: Air (intellectual)
Mode: Mutable (experimenting)

- Experience brought to personality: Exploration
- Contribution made through this sign : Connections and communication

The energy of Gemini is:

- Adaptable: Always open to being influenced by new experiences
- Alert: Interested in the unknown
- Expressive: Interested to invite response and exchange
- Humane: Tolerant of differences and not inclined to prejudge
- Fast-moving: On every level
- Assimilative: Always ready to learn something new
- Contemporaneous: Ready to move on with the times
- Superficial: Not wanting to spend time with any one thing
- Careless of detail: Having too many distractions

The key to understanding the expression of Gemini is that it is communicative, moving between the known and the unknown.

Of Gemini, *Esoteric Astrology* says:

- "And the Word said: Let instability do its work." *(Ordinary man)*
- "I recognise my other self and in the waning of that self I grow and glow." *(Developed man)*

Cancer: The Crab

A polarity with Capricorn
Element: Water (emotional)
Mode: Cardinal (initiating)

- Experience brought to the personality: Awareness of the past
- Contribution made through this sign: New forms to bring through the past

The energy of Cancer is:

- Psychically sensitive: Picks up the memory held in objects, buildings, and places
- Instinctive: Informed by collective experience
- Conditioned by the past: Values what has been
- Seeking identity in origins: Nationalistic, clannish
- Concerned with continuity on all levels: Preservation and procreation
- Protective and nurturing: Supportive of all life forms
- Self-defensive
- Moody
- Immature

The key to understanding the expression of Cancer is the concern
with perpetuation and keeping alive the past.

Of Cancer, *Esoteric Astrology* says:

- "I build a lighted house and therein dwell." *(Ordinary man)*
- "Let isolation be the rule and yet - the crowd exists." *(Developed man)*

Leo: The Lion

♌

A polarity with Aquarius
Element: Fire (spirited)
Mode: Fixed (persevering)

- Experience brought to the personality: That of having individuality
- Contribution made through this sign: Warmth, love, and vitality

The energy of Leo is:

- Commanding of attention: Consciously creates an impression
- Life-affirming: Puts effort into finding enjoyment in living
- Creative: Especially through the medium of performance
- Loving: Willing to give in return for what it desires for itself

- Generous: Likes abundance
- Proud: The pride is in being
- Demanding
- Self-centred
- Self-pitying and self-dramatising

The key to understanding the expression of Leo is the need for personal uniqueness to be recognised by others.

Of Leo, *Esoteric Astrology* says:

- "And the Word said: Let other forms exist. I rule because I am." *(Ordinary man)*
- "I am That and That am I." *(Developed man)*

Virgo: The Maiden

♍

A polarity with Pisces

Element: Earth (material)
Mode: Mutable (experimenting)

- Experience brought to the personality: Awareness of detail
  - Contribution made through this sign: Service

The energy of Virgo is:

- Analytical: On all levels
- Exacting: Of self and others
- Practical: Does not willingly theorise or speculate
- Orderly: Likes cleanliness, tidiness, and good health
- Dutiful: Likes to be helpful
- Modest: Does not seek attention
- Critical: Sees only flaws and imperfections
- Obsessed with detail: Losing the spirit of a law in its letter
- Hypochrondriacal: Focused on the manifestations of illness rather than the cause

The key to understanding the expression of Virgo is the need to be useful to others

Of Virgo, *Esoteric Astrology* says:

- "And the Word said: Let Matter reign." *(Ordinary man)*
- "I am the mother and the child, I, God, I matter am." *(Developed man)*

Libra: The Scales

⎯

A polarity with Aries
Element: Air (intellectual)
Mode: Cardinal (initiating)

- Experience brought to the personality: Awareness of others
- Contribution made through this sign: Awareness of the need for balance

The energy of Libra is:

- Receptive to others: On all levels
- Promoting harmony: Dislikes friction and discord
- Seeking equilibrium: Both inwardly and with reference to external situations
- Responsive: To the concept of justice
- Theoretical: Thinks in terms of principles and abstractions
- Idealistic: Particularly in respect of relationships
- Dissembling: Usually to avoid giving offence
- Self-contradictory: Swayed by the opinions and views of others
- Fearful of unpopularity: Perceives unpopularityas a failure

The key to understanding the expression of Libra is the need to
be on the side of what is perceived to be progressive.

Of Libra, *Esoteric Astrology* says:

- "And the Word said: Let choice be made." *(Ordinary man)*
- "I choose the way that leads between two great lines of force." *(Developed man)*

Scorpio: The Scorpion

♏

A polarity with Taurus
Element:
Water (emotional)
Mode: Fixed (persevering)

- Experience brought to the personality: Understanding of the power of emotion.
- Contribution made by this sign: Awareness

The energy of Scorpio is:

- Psychically sensitive
- Psychically powerful
- Spiritually aware
- Transformative: Of self and others
- Able to make the unconscious conscious
- Combative: Competitive and defensive
- Dominating and controlling: Openly and covertly
- Retentive: On all levels
- Cruel: Mentally and emotionally

The key to understanding the expression of Scorpio is the fear of defeat on the emotional level, leading to rejection and suffering.

Of Scorpio, *Esoteric Astrology* says:

- "And the Word said: Let Maya Flourish and let deception rule." *(Ordinary man)*
- "Warrior I am and from the battle I emerge triumphant." *(Developed man)*

Sagittarius: The Archer

♐

A polarity with Gemini
Element: Fire (spirited)
Mode: Mutable (experimenting)

- Experience brought to the personality: Awareness of a higher level

- Contribution made by this sign: Synthesis of higher and lower

The energy of Sagittarius is:

- Vital: Physically boisterous
- Adventurous: Mentally and physically
- Questioning and curious: Questing
- Open-minded: Stimulated by variety and difference
- Assimilating: Mentally receptive
- Dissatisfied: With all forms of limitation and constraint
- Acquisitive of knowledge
- Clumsy: Emotionally and physically
- Selfish and insensitive to others

The key to understanding the expression of Sagittarius is its need to find purpose.

Of Sagittarius, *Esoteric Astrology* says:

- "And the Word said: Let food be sought." *(Ordinary man)*
- "I see the goal, I reach that goal, and then I see another." *(Developed man)*

Capricorn: The Goat

♑

A pola rity with Cancer
Element: Earth (material)
Mode : Cardinal (initiating)

- Experience brought to the personality: Awareness of cause and effect
- Contribution made by this sign: Practical sense and responsibility

The energy of Capricorn is:

- Hard-working and responsible
- Disciplined
- Realistic
- Ambitious: To rise higher
- Constructive
- Cautious
- Pessimistic

- Inflexible: On all levels
- Materialistic

> The key to understanding the expression of Capricorn is the need for
> control over its resources: spiritual, emotional, and physical.

Of Capricorn, *Esoteric Astrology* says:

- "And the Word said: Let ambition rule and let the door stand wide." *(Ordinary man)*.
- "Lost I am in light supernal, yet on that light I turn my back." *(Developed man)*

Aquarius: The Water-Bearer

♒

A polarity with Leo
Element: Air (intellectual)
Mode: Fixed (persevering)

- Experience brought to the personality: Awareness of the collective
- Contribution made by this sign: Vision that leads to reform.

The energy of Aquarius is:

- Sociable: Likes group activities and movements
- Unconventional: Both personally and in terms of areas of interest
- Inventive and visionary
- Theoretical: Likes principles and projections
- Forward-looking:
- Goal-oriented: Likes to make plans even if they are frequently abandoned
- Ill-disciplined: Scornful of conventional ways of doing things
- Over-talkative: Uses words (form) to the detriment of action and application
- Under-achieving: Fails to deliver

> The key to understanding the expression of Aquarius is the urge
> to find a place in a larger and more significant context.

Of Aquarius, *Esoteric Astrology* says:

- "And the Word said: let desire in form be the ruler." *(Ordinary man)*
- "Water of Life I am, poured forth for thirsty men." *(Developed man)*

Pisces: The Fishes

♓

A polarity with Virgo
Element: Water (emotional)
Mode: Mutable (experimenting)

- The experience brought to the personality: Merging with others
  - The contribution made by this sign: The higher vision

The energy of Pisces is:

- Psychically sensitive
- Forgiving: Accepting of variety and difference
- Self-sacrificing: Does not think solely of the interests of the separated self
- Compassionate: Responsive to the needs of all other sensate beings
- Mystical: Able to lose self in a higher reality
- Visionary: Not restricted by personal reality
- Sad: Bogged down by the suffering in the world
- Ill-disciplined: Indulgent with self and others
- Escapist

The key to understanding the expression of Pisces is the desire to escape personality consciousness and merge with the soul.

Of Pisces, *Esoteric Astrology* says:

- "And the Word said: Go forth into matter." *(Ordinary man)*
- "I leave the Father's Home and turning back, I save." *(Developed man)*

Part Two

Horoscopy's Structure

Chapter 5

Preparing to Work with the Zodiacal Signs

We all start a study of astrology from where we stand. How we understand and use the language of astrology is determined by our own level of awareness. As that expands, so our understanding of astrology will gain in breadth and depth. For this reason, it is not desirable to see astrology as a finite body of knowledge that can be acquired. What can be learned is an approach to the use of the language of astrology; that involves finding a way of working that is comfortable and authentic. None of us do good work for as long as we are using concepts that we do not understand or of which we do not see the point. Never be afraid to carve out your own niche in this potentially limitless discipline, using only those ideas that make sense to you and that you yourself find helpful.

***

In this section, we are offering an approach to working with the signs of the zodiac. The comments made here apply to all the twelve signs.

The Decanates

In Chapter Three, we described the signs as zones of influence that have a conditioning effect upon the planets that move into them, and we noted that each sign comprises three decanates or subzones, each of ten degrees.

Each decanate is ruled by a planet. These rulers will be identified in Part Three of this work, which is given over to a study of the planets.

- The first decanate of a sign corresponds to the first principle: life. The energy in this subzone encourages the planet within it to express itself in an outer-directed way. A person with a lot of planets in the first decanate of signs could be expected to be action-oriented and focused upon serving his own interests.
- The second decanate of a sign corresponds to the second principle: quality. The energy in this subzone encourages a planet to express itself in a more thoughtful and reflective

way. A person with a lot of planets in the second decanate of signs could be expected to be concerned with understanding himself through his interactions with others.

- The third decanate of a sign corresponds to the third principle: appearance or fusion. This encourages a planet within it to present itself in a purposeful way. A person with a lot of planets in the third decanate of signs could be expected to be engaged in finding and fulfilling his purpose, which is an expression of his relationship (fusion) with a higher level.

The Signs and the Planets

The planets take into each sign their own essential nature, and the result is a blend of energies. Sign + planet = 2. Esoterically considered, two is the number of consciousness. This means that we express this blend of energy relatively consciously (i.e. we are aware that we are expressing ourselves in this kind of way).

The hyleg points, however, are said in the language of conventional astrology to "cast no rays" (i.e. to emit no influence of their own). This means that there is no blending ingredient (sign + hyleg = 1), so we are less conscious of the energy that comes through a hyleg point. Because we are identified with them, these energies act in our lives in a way that we often do not recognise, and because of this, they manifest themselves in a qualitatively different way.

For example, a person with the sign Libra on the ascendant is compulsively and automatically agreeable and accommodating of others, whereas a person with Sun in Libra intentionally espouses values that promote balance and justice. This is an important distinction.

The Signs and the Ascendant (The Rising Sign)

Let us recapitulate what we have noted about the ascendant so far:

- It always appears on the left side of the chart.
- It is the eastern point of interception of the ecliptic and the rational horizon.

If the ecliptic is a circle, which is split into twelve zodiacal zones, the point of interception will be a specific degree within a decanate within a sign. These are known as the rising degree and rising sign.

The ecliptic moves at a rate that brings a new degree to the point of interception approximately every four minutes. (Hence, the importance of strict accuracy in the matter of birth time.) Over a twenty-four hour period, all 360 degrees of the zodiac will have occupied that point of interception.

Most people who are interested in astrology understand that the ascendant is in some way connected to the soul, even if they do not understand why.

The rising degree (the point of interception between the ecliptic and the rational horizon) represents the point of entry (i.e. the crown chakra) of the life force into the etheric body of a human being.

It represents the point at which the individual human being receives the life force via the collectively that is the human soul. It is down-flowing energy (first principle: life) that expresses itself in accordance with the sign and decanate to which the rising degree belongs.

The ascendant is, therefore, the point of interface between the separated human personality and the human soul that bestows life. Understanding the quality of the connection (i.e. the zodiacal sign) is a key to understanding the life because it describes the energy the soul is using the personality to manifest on the material plane.

When consciousness (second principle) is brought to bear on this connection, it promotes fusion (third principle) of the soul and personality.

We will look at this matter again in the chapters that focus upon the houses. Here we are concerned with the ascendant as a conduit for zodiacal energy.

The Signs and the MC

- The MC is the most elevated point on a chart. It is in the south of the map.
- The MC is the point of interception between the ecliptic and the meridian.
- The MC represents the culmination point of what appears to be the Sun's daily ascent to the observer on Earth.

In a natal chart, the MC represents the highest energy centre in the personality vehicle: the throat chakra. The higher chakras, situated in the head, are considered to belong to the soul.

The MC, therefore, describes by sign and decanate the energy that is drawing the personality on and what represents progress for him. This energy, like that of the ascendant, may be expressed unconsciously, or it may be something that we come to understand very thoroughly (second principle: consciousness) and incorporate into our lives, through our choice of career and lifestyle (third principle: appearance or fusion).

Chapter 6

Introducing the Houses

Astrologers tend to get very partisan about the house system they use and are inclined to defend it hotly, even though, in fact, they probably do not understand the technical differences between their system and any other. What they are saying is that that system works for them. This is a most persuasive testimony, but it is not the same as saying that another might not if they were to work with it over time. Don't get stuck in angst about the house systems: You have a better use for your time! This matter is a problem in modern Western astrology only until astrologers discover from direct experience that it does not need to be.

***

When we look through a window, we see a view, but we see also the frame of the window. We see the view through that frame and only as much of what is beyond it as the frame permits. The window frame is the structure that contains and defines the view. So it is with the astrological houses, which may be likened to twelve windows, each looking out on the ecliptic from the place of birth. Each of those windows corresponds to an area of life. When a planet is visible through a window, its influence will be working through that frame.

Collectively, these twelve frames encompass the areas of life or categories of experience that make up our modern day realities. We will look at each house in more detail later in this lesson.

In the table below, we give a basic description.

House	Area of Life
First 1	Physical appearance
Second 2	Values
Third 3	Conditioning environment
Fourth 4	Personal past
Fifth 5	Creativity
Sixth 6	Vocation & health
Seventh 7	Relationships
Eighth 8	Emotional experience

Ninth 9	Spiritual quest
Tenth 10	Ambitions and goals
Eleventh11	Fellowship
Twelfth 12	Merging

We are all influenced by the Sun, the Moon, and the planets, but the windows through which those influences come into us will condition their expression. In turn, this will determine our experiences within those areas of life and influence the way that we understand them. This is why two people with the same Sun sign can be so different in the way that they manifest that energy.

So far so good, but how do we construct these twelve windows? Clearly, we do not see them with our physical sight any more than we see a cartographic grid on a landscape.

The houses are a device used by astrologers for locating planets. They are not the only device; in Part One, we noted how the planets position on the ecliptic was measured by celestial longitude and celestial latitude. In fact, the houses are a secondary location.

- First, the planets are located in zodiacal signs, which are the twelve zones of the ecliptic.
- Second, they are in the houses that represent the twelve areas of human experience, which overlay the ecliptic as a window frame superimposes itself on a view.

The houses represent terrestrial level, a lower level than that of the heavens, but there is correspondence between these two levels.

The House System Controversy

The means for constructing the house frame are the tables of houses of which there are many different versions. Western astrologers tend to argue about the relative merits of the principal three or four systems, but in fact, there are numerous systems for creating twelve windows out to the heavens from the place of birth, and each makes the houses a slightly different size.

It is too much for the student new to astrology to follow the theory behind these systems, and on becoming aware of the house system controversy, a student frequently feels confused and disillusioned because the lack of consensus in a matter so central to the construction of a horoscope appears to call into question the validity of astrology, and certainly the claims that it is a science.

Any student disorientated by the house system controversy is advised to simply push ahead using one system, and then, when there is a greater familiarity with the craft, to explore other house systems, letting their own findings decide the matter. The chances are they will find merits in most of them and certainly they will have lost any misgivings that they might have had about the house system controversy invalidating horoscopy. Astrology is not a science; it is a vehicle for bringing through a higher level of consciousness. Different considerations apply.

In this work, we focus upon three systems:

- Placidus: It is still the most widely used system.
- Koch: This system is popular with event-oriented astrologers who play close attention to planetary activity at the house cusps (Endnote 1)
- Equal house: It will eventually be used with the sidereal zodiac to become the house system of esoteric astrology. In this work, we use it with the tropical zodiac, because western consciousness is not yet ready to change over to the sidereal zodiac.

Figures 4, 5, and 6 (below) show Valentine's chart constructed according to the Equal house, Placidus, and Koch systems. Students should look at the degrees on the cusps of the twelve houses and note the differences and similarities, paying particularly close attention to the degrees of the hylegs. They should also observe what these differences do to the distribution of the planets.

The important thing for the beginner to appreciate is that, while the various house systems may make the houses different sizes, the significance of each of the houses is not affected. The first house, for example, is still the house of appearance and still governs the physical appearance and whether we use Koch, Placid us, or any other system.

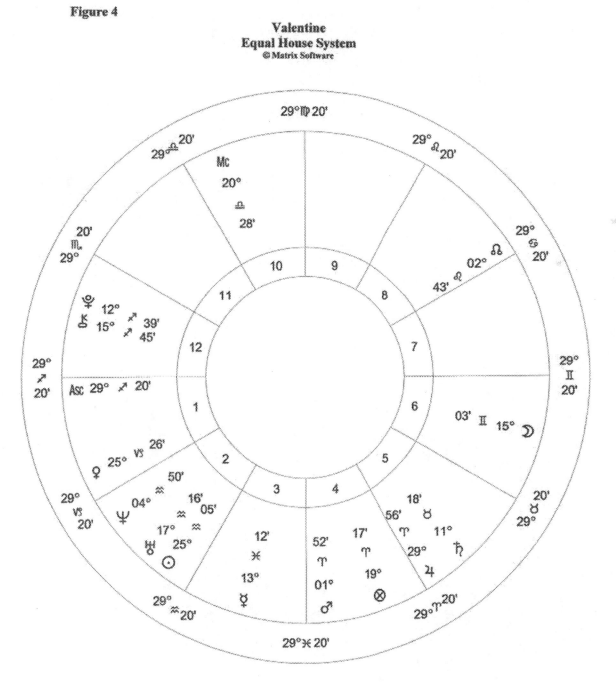

Figure 4

Valentine
Equal House System
© Matrix Software

Figure 5

Valentine
Placidus House System
© Matrix Software

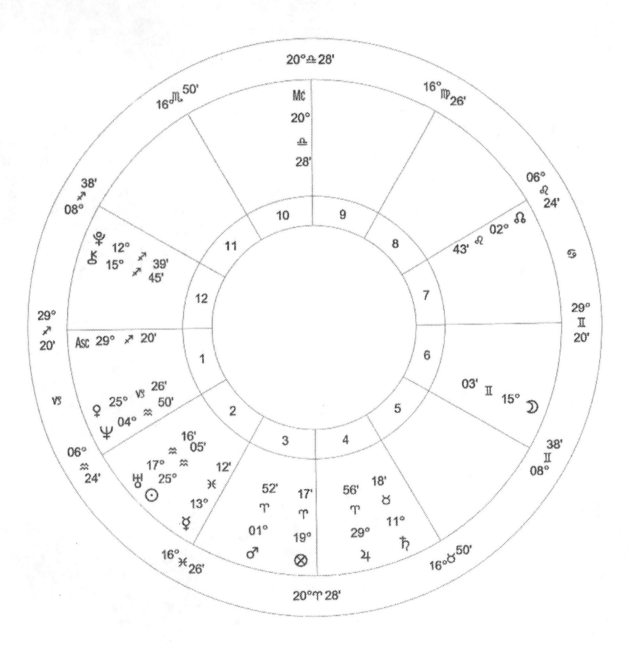

Figure 6

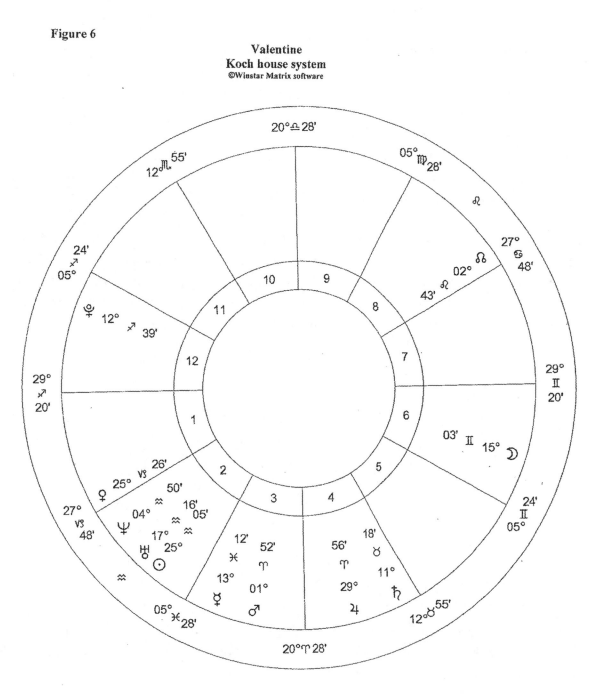

Valentine
Koch house system
©Winstar Matrix software

Understanding the Houses

The houses are numbered one to twelve, starting with the house directly below the ascendant and working counterclockwise. It is convenient, as noted earlier, to think about the houses as "areas of life."

The twelve houses comprise six polarities:

- Opposite house twelve is house six
- Opposite house eleven is house five
- Opposite house one is house seven
- Opposite house two is house eight
- Opposite house three is house nine
- Opposite house ten is house four

Each of the twelve houses corresponds to one of the twelve signs of the zodiac: It is considered that this area of life manifests in accordance with the quality of the zodiacal sign to which is corresponds (eg, the eleventh house is the house of fellowship and ideals, and it corresponds to the sign Aquarius, the symbol of which is the water carrier). Uranus, the ruler of the sign Aquarius, is said to be the "natural ruler" of the eleventh house

House	Corresponds to	Natural Planetary Ruler
First	Aries	Mars
Second	Taurus	Venus
Third	Gemini	Mercury
Fourth	Cancer	Moon
Fifth	Leo	Sun
Sixth	Virgo	Mercury
Seventh	Libra	Venus
Eighth	Scorpio	Mars and Pluto
Ninth	Sagittarius	Jupiter
Tenth	Capricorn	Saturn
Eleventh	Aquarius	Saturn and Uranus
Twelfth	Pisces	Jupiter and Neptune

The houses are a frame into which all forms of life can be fitted, including the parts of the human anatomy. The contribution of modem Western astrology has been to add to this, listing nonphysical human attributes (emotional, mental, and spiritual states).

Thus, in Western astrology, the eleventh house, the house of fellowship, governs specific friends, which a person has and the groups to which he belongs, but it also governs the urge to join forces with others and the idealism and vision that inspire and inform group activity. It also governs the pituitary gland, which permits the consciousness of unity and the parts of the body (i.e. the calves and ankles that are related to the pituitary body). People who have done yoga will be aware that the pituitary gland can be stimulated by exercises to the lower leg (Endnote 2).

Grouping the houses

The twelve houses, like the twelve signs, are put into different categories and the nature of the category will condition the expression of the luminaries and planets that fall into these houses.

Conventional astrology recognises two principal groupings, although many contemporary astrologers may be unfamiliar with them. This is a reflection of the fact that people now learn astrology less thoroughly; it is not a comment upon the usefulness of the concepts.

The first of these conventional groupings is as follows:

> Individual: houses one, five, and nine
> Temporal: houses two, six, and ten
> Relative: houses three, seven, and eleven
> Terminal: houses four, eight, and twelve

If we look at the list of natural rulers, we will see that:

- Individual houses are those whose natural rulers are the fire signs, and they relate to a person's body (house one/Aries), soul, (house five/Leo), and spirit (house nine/Sagittarius) (i.e. his composition).
- Temporal houses are those whose natural rulers are the earth signs, and they relate to a person's possessions (house two/Taurus), health and personal capacity (house six/Virgo), and career or lifestyle (house ten/Capricorn) (i.e. his acquisitions).
- Relative houses are those whose natural rulers are the air signs, and they relate to a
- person's siblings and kin (house three/Gemini), partners (house seven/Libra), and friends (house eleven/Aquarius) (i.e. his associations).
- Terminal houses are those whose natural rulers are the water signs, and they relate to
- a person's sense of connection to this family and country (house four/Cancer), to his sense of connection to those with whom he has emotional and sexual ties (house eight/Scorpio), and to his sense of being connected to a higher level (house twelve/Pisces) (i.e. his sense of who he is/his identity).

If the term *terminal* causes confusion, think of these houses as being the end or conclusion of certain kind experiences

The second of these conventional groupings is as follows:

Angular: houses one, four, seven, and ten
Succedent: houses two, five, eight, and eleven
Cadent: houses three, six, nine, and twelve

Although this way of classifying, like the previous one, has fallen out of favour with modern astrology, it has many merits because the awareness behind it anticipates a more esoteric grouping known as the Crosses of the Heavens (Endnote 3)

For now, it is necessary to understand only that the influence through:

- The angular houses are energising and action-orientated and is expressive of life.
- The succedent houses are consolidating and acquisitive and is expressive of quality.
- The cadent houses are fluid and experimental and are expressive of appearance: the fusion of personality and soul.

It may be evident that the first grouping (individual, temporal, relative, and terminal) corresponds to the grouping of the signs by element and describes their quality. The second grouping (angular, succedent, and cadent) corresponds to the grouping of the signs by modality and describes their mode of expression.

The concept of the areas of consciousness absorbs and extends the ideas contained in the previous two groupings

- Area of personal consciousness: houses one, two, three, and four
- Area of relating consciousness: houses five, six, seven, and eight
- Area of universal consciousness: houses nine, ten, eleven, and twelve

- The area of personal consciousness develops awareness of self and builds the personal reality. Planets working through these houses are self-serving and selfdefining in their effect.
- The area of relating consciousness develops awareness of other. Planets working through these houses make relationships with others of extreme importance to self definition and the expression of identity.
- The area of universal consciousness develops awareness of the group, which is the lower correspondence of the soul. Planets working through these houses make joining forces with organisations, groups, and causes of extreme importance to self-definition and the expression of identity.

With this frame in place, we can find more meaning in the previous groupings:

Area of consciousness: Personal
Function: Creating awareness of the separated self and its capacities

The term *emphasised* below should be taken to mean containing the Sun or the Moon or a number of inner planets.

House	Corresponds to:	Grouping	Comments
First *Appearance*	Aries	Individual *I* Angular	Corresponds to the fire signs and to the cardinal modality. With this house emphasised, a person asserts himself with much energy to make his mark on the world and to learn from the experience of being persppersonally effective
Second *Values*	Taurus	Temporal *I* Succedent	Corresponds to the earth signs and the fixed modality. With this house emphasised, a person is concerned with acquisition and consolidation. He needs to be able to externalise his own value system.

| Third *Conditioning environment* | Gemini | Relative *I* Cadent | Corresponds to the air signs and the mutable modality. With this house emphasised, a person is concerned with communication and the exchange of ideas. He needs to interact with others in order to know himself. |
| Fourth *Personal past* | Cancer | Terminal *I* Angular | Corresponds to the water signs and the cardinal modality. With this house emphasised, a person is concerned with the matter of continuity. He needs to understand what has made him who he is (his personal past) and is concerned to pass on to his children what he considers to be of value. |

Area of consciousness: Relative
Function: Creating awareness of others and giving experiences in cooperation and sharing

Fifth *Creativity*	Leo	Individual *I* Succedent	Corresponds to the fire signs and the fixed modality. With this house emphasised, a person is concerned with creative expression and the gaining of recognition from others.
Sixth *Vocation and health*	Virgo	Temporal *I* Cadent	Corresponds to the earth signs and the mutable modality. With this house emphasised, a person is concerned with his physical vehicle from the point of view of its health and the service that he can render with it.
Seventh *Relationships*	Libra	Relative *I* Angular	Corresponds to the air signs and the cardinal modality. With this house emphasised, a person is concerned with defining himself through his relationships, his approach to which is influenced by theories and concepts of relating.

Eighth *Emotional experience*	Scorpio	Terminal *I* Succedent	Corresponds to the water signs and the fixed modality. With this house Emphasised, a person is concerned upon his emotional reactions to his dealings with others and with the learning of sympathy and compassion.

Area of consciousness: Universal
Function: Creating awareness of the group which is the lower correspondence of the soul

Ninth *Spiritual quest*	Sagittarius	Individual *I* Cadent	Corresponds to the fire signs and the mutable modality. With this house emphasised, a person is concerned with understanding his place in the larger scheme of things by exploring the world of form, be that through geographical travel or intellectual pursuits.
Tenth *Ambitions and goals*	Capricorn	Temporal *I* Angular	Corresponds to the earth signs and the cardinal modality. With this house emphasised, a person is ambitious and goal-orientated, be his goals those of wordly success or spiritual attainment.

Eleventh *Fellowship*	Aquarius	Relative *I* Succedent	Corresponds to the air signs and the fixed modality. With this house emphasised, a person is idealistic and inclined toward group activities.
Twelfth *Absorption*	Pisces	Terminal *I* Cadent	Corresponds to the water signs and the mutable modality. With this house emphasised, a person is aware of a higher reality (the plane of the soul) to which he yearns to return.

Students are advised to study their own natal charts and list the houses that contain planets, categorising them by:

- Sign correspondence
- Natural ruler
- Area of consciousness
- Grouping

Endnotes

1. A more technical presentation of the differences is beyond the scope of this work, but in his introduction to *The Michelsen Book of Tables*, Robert Hand outlines the differences between Koch and Placidus while making it clear that he does not consider that there is, as yet, enough, if any, research-based evidence that recommends one over the other.

2. During the 1970s and 1980s, when astrology was incorporating the language of psychology, there was a turning away from form in favour of using the houses to delineate states of mind and psychological conditions. This practice is not necessarily helpful: How does a person discover that he has a psychological problem about joining forces with others if not by difficulties experienced in specific friendships and in specific groups? In the practice of astrology, it is very important that the astrologer can start with the client at the place in everyday life where a situation is manifesting and trace it inward. There are few things less helpful than being too lofty and too abstract.

3. The Cross of the Heavens is covered in some detail in this author's book *Transitional Astrology*.

Chapter 7

House Profiles

The astrological houses are areas of the psyche, parts of the body and categories into which we place all that we perceive to be out there: people, animals, and things. When we understand this, we begin to understand how we make our own realities. The horoscope is a map of the mind.

✳✳✳

First House

♈ House of Aries; natural ruler: Mars ♂

Consciousness developed by experiences in this house: awareness through self-assertion & personal effectiveness

The luminaries & planets in this house condition: self-confidence - sense of personal empowerment - capacity to act

The zodiacal sign on the cusp of this house describes: the way in which a person approaches this area of life.

This house governs: persona - self-image - physical appearance in general - head and face specifically

Second House

♉ House of Taurus; natural ruler: Venus ♀

Consciousness developed by experiences in this house: awareness through acquisition and material consolidation

The luminaries & planets in this house condition: ability to handle money & resources - attitude to giving

The zodiacal sign on the cusp of this house describes: a person's value system and priorities.

This house governs: values - personal resources - money & possessions - the throat & neck

Third House

♊ **House of Gemini; natural ruler: Mercury** ☿

Consciousness developed by experiences in this house: awareness of personal reality through communication and cultural influences

The luminaries & planets in this house condition: ability to define personal reality - powers of communication - intellectual capacity - relationship to kin

The zodiacal sign on the cusp of this house describes: the approach to learning and the perceived purpose of communication

This house governs: The rational mind - the separated reality of the personality - the written & spoken word - education & places of learning - the environment - inland travel - transport - the siblings - the hands, arms and shoulders

Fourth House

♋ **House of Cancer; natural ruler: Moon** ☽

Consciousness developed by experiences in this house: awareness through the experience of perpetuation and continuity (most obviously expressed through the parental relationship)

The luminaries & planets in this house condition: sense of connectedness to the past - the childhood experiences - the relationship to the mother - the ability to create a home in adult life - relationship to property

The zodiacal sign on the cusp of this house describes: the energetic quality of the mother - the attitude to self-discovery - the attitude to the home

This house governs: Link to the collective unconscious - the personal past - the childhood - the mother & motherhood - the country of birth (motherland) - the home, real estate - the breasts and upper stomach

Fifth House

♌ **House of Leo; natural ruler: Sun** ☉

Consciousness developed by experiences in this house: awareness through the expressing of creativity and individuality

The luminaries & planets in this house condition: creative potency - attitude to the value of personal creative contribution - self-valuation

The zodiacal sign on the cusp of this house describes : the kind of expression that will best suit the creative capacity

This house governs: individuality - creativity - sexual expression - conception of children - recreation - the heart

Sixth House

♍ **House of Virgo; natural ruler: Mercury** ☿

Consciousness developed by experiences in this house: awareness through the expression of function & execution of duty

The luminaries & planets in this house condition: attitudes to work - the willingness to serve - the state of the health - attitude to animals

The zodiacal sign on the cusp of this house describes : the perceived purpose of work - attitude to physicality

This house governs: Work - vocation - health - domestic pets - lower stomach

Seventh House

♎ **House of Libra: natural ruler: Venus** ♀

Consciousness developed by experiences in this house: awareness through experience in personal relationships

The luminaries & planets in this house condition: the requirement of relationships - the energies sought from the partner - the experience in relationships

The zodiacal sign on the cusp of this house describes: the experience sought through relationship - the perceived purpose of relationship

This house governs: relationship - balance - partnerships with commitment - kidneys

Eighth House

♏ **House of Scorpio; natural ruler: Mars / Pluto** ♂/♀

Consciousness developed by experiences in this house: awareness through losing self in other

The luminaries & planets in this house condition: emotional and sexual dealings with others - the way a person is treated by those close to him -atunement to the astral plane

The zodiacal sign on the cusp of this house describes: the quality and purpose of experience sought through emotional and sexual involvement

This house governs: desire - sexual union - sympathy - death - astral entities - shared resources - reproductive organs & bowels

Ninth House

♐ **House of Sagittarius; natural ruler: Jupiter** ♃

Consciousness developed by experiences in this house: awareness through the quest for meaning

The luminaries and planets in this house condition: interest in spirituality - curiosity about the unknown - attitude to pushing out boundaries mentally and physically

The zodiacal sign on the cusp of this house describes : the nature and form of the spirituality

This house governs: higher knowledge - religion & law - other countries and cultures - overseas travel - the hips & thighs

Tenth House

♑ **House of Capricorn; natural ruler: Saturn** ♄

Consciousness developed by experiences in this house: awareness though pursuing goals and working for recognition

The luminaries & planets in this house condition: attitudes to authority and to established order - relationship with the father and the fatherland - capacity to pursue goals

The zodiacal sign on the cusp of this house describes: orientation of the life and the structure of the lifestyle

This house governs: authority - the Establishment - the state - the father - the career - the knees

Eleventh House

♒ **House of Aquarius: natural ruler: Saturn /Uranus** ♄/♅

Consciousness developed by experiences in this house: awareness through fellowship and communal endeavour

The luminaries & Planets in this house condition: the attitude to group activity - approach to friendship - the way of interacting with others in a group setting - the attitude towards working to bring about change

The zodiacal sign on the cusp of this house describes: the motivation for joining forces with others

This house governs: ideals - fellowship - friends - communal activities - groups - children after birth (the next generation) - the calves and ankle

Twelfth House

♓ **House of Pisces; natural ruler: Jupiter / Neptune** ♃/♆

Consciousness developed by experiences in this house: awareness through the experience of non-separation

The luminaries & Planets in this house condition: attunement to the soul plane - inspiration - ability to lose self-centredness

The zodiacal sign on the cusp of this house describes: the energy and circumstances (including challenges issued to the personality) required to attune to a higher level

This house governs: compassion - self transcendence - physical restriction seclusion - places of retreat - the feet

Part Three

The Planets

Chapter 8

The Planets of Our Solar System

Although they represent different lines of enquiry, astrology and astronomy are not wholly divorced. To have some understanding of the physical features of each planet will benefit the astrologer because the esotericist knows that the physical features are expressive of the inner reality. Thus Jupiter, the largest planet in the solar system, represents the principle of expansion to the astrologer. Mars, the red planet, represents the principle of passion and assertion. To an astrologer, a basic astronomy book about the solar system, even one written for children, can be a very useful tool.

***

Let us remind ourselves of what was said in Chapter Two about the role of the planets in the distribution of force in our solar system

- The planets receive energy from outside our solar system, the constellations, and return processed energy in the form of consciousness to the Sun .
- The Sun gives that energy back to the planets.
- The planets give energy to organic life living on the surface of our planet.
- Organic life on Earth processes it and either sends it on to the Moon or sends it back (up) to the planets in the form of consciousness.

Distribution of energy in our solar system: Involutionary

Constellations of the Milky Way
Sun
Planets
Organic life on Earth, including unconscious humanity
Earth
Moon

We noted how the human kingdom is the variable factor in nature's distribution arrangements. If a man is conscious and lives consciously, the energy he generates will be of a high enough quality to be returned to the planets.

Raising the level of the energy that we transform, whilst in incarnation, is the basic purpose being served by the spiritual and religious systems that encourage us to live consciously, and it is this purpose that the esoteric astrologer serves. We tend to think in terms of our spirituality serving our needs, but, our spirituality serves the purposes of our planet, too.

Distribution of energy in our solar system with a conscious participation from the human kingdom: Evolutionary

Constellations of the Milky Way
Sun
Planets
Organic life on Earth
Conscious humanity
Planets

According to *The Secret Doctrine* (Endnote 1), there are a total of seventy planets in our solar system that influence the destiny of nations. Contemporary astrology is built around just two luminaries and eight planets. This indicates the scope that exists for the astrology of the future.

Unlike the stars, which are gaseous and self-illuminating, the planets are dense matter and reflect the light of the Sun. They have no light of their own.

This is a matter of considerable significance to the esoteric astrologer, because reflection is the way that a higher level of consciousness communicates to the lower that could not otherwise bear the brilliance of its light.

Being gaseous and self-illuminating, the Sun belongs to the stellar and not the planetary world, a consideration that is also of importance to the astrologer.

Orbital motion

The planets, of course, orbit the Sun, and as they do so, they rotate upon their axes. Although astrology records the orbital movement of the planets, planetary axial rotation is not a factor of any significance in modern astrology. The exception to this is Earth's own axial rotation because this gives us the house system and what are called *directions*, which belong to more advanced astrology.

However, it is worth knowing that:

- It is axial rotation that accounts for the fact that we cannot see the dark side of the Moon from the Earth. Earth and its satellite rotate face to face, as it were.
- The same is true of the Sun and Mercury, which also rotate face to face.
- The Sun, as it rotates (west to east), orbits the point that we call the Galactic Centre, which, from the point of view of the observer on Earth, is situated in the sign Sagittarius.
- Whilst the other planets rotate east to west, Uranus and the Earth rotate west to east.

The Moon, Mercury, and Venus have orbits which bring them between Earth and the Sun. For this reason, they are often called the inner planets.

Earth is contained within the orbit of all the other planets.

Celestial body	Mean distance from Sun in millions of miles	sidereal period*	rank in terms of speed of motion	retrograde motion
Mercury	36	88 days	2	
Venus	67.2	224.7	3	
the Sun / Earth **	93	365 days	4	x
Mars	141.5	687 days	5	
Jupiter	483.3	12 years	6	
Saturn	886.1	29.46 years	7	
Chiron***	1,330	50 years	8	
Uranus	1,783	84 years	9	
Neptune	2,797	164.8 years	10	
Pluto	3,670	248.4 years	11	
Moon	238.9 thousand miles from Earth	27.4 days	1	x

* Time taken to orbit the Sun
** The Great Illusion, as it is known, creates the appearance that we know so well of the Sun moving around the Earth and the motional habits of the Earth are projected onto the Sun. Thus, to the astrologer as to the observer on Earth, it is *the Sun* that appears to take 365 days to move through the zodiac.
*** Not known to conventional astrology but now gaining acceptance.

The Great Illusion, as it is known, creates the appearance of the Sun moving around Earth and the motional habits of Earth are projected onto the Sun . Thus, to the astrologer as to the observer on Earth, it is the Sun that appears to take 365 days to move through the zodiac.

Planetary motion

The speed of motion is of defining importance to the astrologer when it comes to assessing the relative strength of the planets. It is essential, therefore, that this ranking be learned and an awareness gained of the speed of each planet relative to the others.

The rule in astrology is that the slower the motion of a planet, the greater its influence.

Based on planetary motion, astrological tradition places the planets in one of three categories. Although these terms are rather old-fashioned and modern astrology prefers to talk about faster and slower moving planets, the conventional categories have their place.

Inferior planets:
Mercury
Venus

Superior planets:
Mars,
Jupiter,
Saturn

Outer planets:
Uranus,
Neptune
Pluto

Chiron, the orbit of which is between Saturn and Uranus, is known as a planetoid, which is a cross between a planet and an asteroid (see Endnote 2).

Retrogradation

All the planets, except the Sun and Moon (and they technically are called luminaries to distinguish them from planets) are seen by the observer on Earth to move backward through the heavens for periods of time that vary from days (in the case of the inferior planets) to months (in the case of the outer planets).

Retrogradation is an optical illusion created by Earth's rotational speed exceeding that of the planets' orbital motion. As the optical illusion is created with reference to Earth, it is irrelevant to talk of Earth itself having retrograde motion. However, we must consider the hypothetical situation in which to any observer on another planet in the solar system, Earth too would be seen to move backward.

According to conventional astrology, when a planet is in retrograde motion, its influence is weakened. An esoterically orientated astrologer knows, however, that it is not weakened so much as redirecting its energy to work on the inner planes rather than the physical plane, affecting the emotional or mental parts of man.

Aspects

Aspects are to be defined as the angular relationship between two planets. These relationships comprise a large part of the language of astrology and are the point of departure between astronomy and astrology.

Astronomy's interest in aspects stops at the gravitational pull of one planet upon another. For the astrologer, however, the aspects provide him with the vocabulary of his chosen language.

Later in this work, we will be looking at the matter of how to read the aspects.

For now, it is important to keep in mind the point made that the slower the motion of the planet, the stronger its influence. The slower planet is said to influence the faster planet, but the faster will express the contact. This statement may take some thinking about.

The nature of that influence will depend upon the quality of the slower planet and angle from which the aspect is thrown.

This means that:

- The Moon is influenced by the Sun and all planets.
- The Sun is influenced by the superior and outer planets but itself influences the inferior planets.
- The superior planets are influenced by the outer planets but themselves influence the Sun and the inner planets.
- The outer planets are influenced only by each other. (Uranus is influenced by Neptune and Pluto, Neptune is influenced by Pluto but influences Uranus, and Pluto receives no influence. It can only influence.)

Endnotes

1. *The Secret Doctrine*, HP Blavatsky, The Theosophical Publishing Company, 1888.

2. Asteriods are the thousands of small bodies, most of which orbit between Mars and Jupiter. They may be the remains of a planet that occupied the same orbit. The first asteroid to be discovered was Ceres in 1801. Chiron, which orbits between Saturn and Uranus, was discovered in 1974 and may have come into our solar system from another galaxy to be only a temporary resident.

Chapter 9

The Planets in the Astrologer's World
Basic Considerations

Students frequently ask what is more important: the sign in which the planet is found or the house through which it operates. For understanding ourselves as we are now and our lives as they are now, the houses are the most important; but for understanding our potential, the signs hold that secret. But, as is ever the case, if we would understand anything thoroughly, we must start from where we stand. We must first come to a thorough understanding of what the planetary energies bring into each of the twelve areas of life or categories that make up our reality.

***

For the astrologer, like the astronomer, the planets and the Sun form our solar system. The astrologer, however, moves on from that point and sees the mind of the personality in incarnation as having a correspondence to the solar system.

Each of us is a system of consciousness, and some astrologers refer to the natal chart the picture of our inner sky. Essentially, the natal chart is a map of the mind.

- The Sun, the principle of self-awareness, is the central organisor.
- The Moon represents the principle of continuity between the past and the present.
- The planets represent different principles of consciousness that it is the task of the Sun to organise into a functioning system.

In this lesson, we are concerned with how the planets fit into the picture that is the natal chart.

The natal chart shows the structure and internal dynamics of the individual's mind.

- The signs in which the luminaries and planets are found describe how that energy will express itself.
- The houses that represent the areas of life show where the energy principles represented by the luminaries and planets will express themselves.

- The relationship that planets have with each other and the luminaries will determine whether they cooperate or interfere with one another, always remembering that the slower moving the planet, the more powerful its influence.

There are, however, conditions that will give any planet additional strength or, conversely, weaken it, although they do not override the rule that the slower influences the faster.

Introducing the planets

Celestial body	Symbol	Representation in astrology
Luminaries:		
Sun	☉	The true identity; the quality of the individuality
Moon	☽	The past; the quality of the past life memory; the mother
Inner or inferior planets:		
Mercury	☿	Communication; the siblings
Venus	♀	Our values: who and what we love
Mars	♂	Our drive; who and what impels us
Superior planets:		
Jupiter	♃	Expansiveness; the area of life in which we are least restricted
Saturn	♄	The mind set; karmic inheritance; the father
Planetoid:		
Chiron	⚷	The 'scar on the soul'; the nature of spiritual difficulties in past life
Outer planets:		
Uranus	♅	Liberation; those things from which the personality must get free

Neptune	Ψ	Absorption of the one into the many; the area of life in which the personality can best understand the perspectives of the soul
Pluto	♀ / ♇	Transformation of the lower into the higher; area of life in which emotional regeneration is required

It is important that the student becomes thoroughly familiar with the planetary symbols and their basic meanings before moving on. Later, we will look at each luminary and planet in more detail.

Planets in Signs

Planets in their own signs

Each planet rules a sign. When it is found in that sign, it is at home and its influence is strong. This means that:

☉ is strong in ♌
☽ is strong in ♋
☿ is strong in ♊, ♍
♀ is strong in ♉, ♎
♂ is strong in ♈, ♏
♃ is strong in ♐, ♓
♄ is strong in ♑, ♒
♅ is strong in ♒
♆ is strong in ♓
♇ is strong in ♏

When a planet is strong in its own sign, it gives a typical expression that, as far as everyday living goes, is not the same as its best expression.

- The Sun in Leo is very aware of itself and may be egotistical and self-important, as well as warm and passionate.
- The Moon in Cancer is very emotional and instinctive, as well as nurturing and feminine.

Planets in their detriment

Planets are said to be in their detriment when they are in a sign opposite that to that which they rule.

⊙ is in its detriment in ♒

☽ is in its detriment in ♑

☿ is in its detriment in ♐

♀ is in its detriment in ♏

♂ is in its detriment in ♎

♃ is in its detriment in ♍

♄ is in its detriment in ♋

The outer planets are not held to be susceptible to detrimental influences.

In the sign of its detriment, the planet does not do its job well and the result is a weak, frequently muddled expression.

- The Sun in Aquarius is unfocused and easily influenced.
- The Moon in Capricorn is materialistic and unemotional.

Planets in exaltation

Planets are said to be in exaltation (or dignified) in the signs that encourage their most positive and constructive expression, and as such, they are of particular importance to the unfolding of the potential of a lifetime. Correctly speaking, the outer planets are said to have an affinity with a sign rather than have a place of exaltation, but this is probably rather pedantic by today's standards.

⊙ is in its exaltation in ♈

☽ is in its exaltation in ♉

☿ is in its exaltation in ♍

♀ is in its exaltation in ♓

♂ is in its exaltation in ♑

♃ is in its exaltation in ♋

♄ is in its exaltation in ♎

♅ has an affinity with ♏

♆ has an affinity with ♌

♇ has an affinity with ♍

- The Sun in Aries is full of life and vitality and strengthens the sense of self.
- The Moon in Taurus is responsible and equable.

Planets in their fall

Planets are said to be in their fall when they occupy signs that absorb them. This is a different concept from detriment where the effect is frustrating. In the sign of their fall, the customary expression ceases to be influential in the unfolding of life. They are said to fade out. The inference is that the planetary principle has now been dealt with adequately within the context of the psyche of a person with a planet in its fall, and this indicates a significant stage in development. Correctly speaking, the outer planets do not fall.

⊙ is in its fall in ♎

☽ is in its fall in ♏

☿ is in its fall in ♓

♀ is in its fall in ♍

♂ is in its fall in ♋

♃ is in its fall in ♑

♄ is in its fall in ♈

- The Sun in Libra is aware of others and the sense of self is held in check by this.
- The Moon in Scorpio is destructive of all that the Moon represents in terms of the hold of the past.

In application, the concepts of a planet in its own sign and a planet in its detriment are largely practical in that they enable an astrologer to identify a planet that is well-placed and powerful and one that is disadvantaged and weak.

The concepts of planets in exaltation and planets in fall have a greater significance in terms of our development and are therefore of special importance to the esoterically oriented astrologer.

Students should examine their own charts, and list all planets in their own signs and in detriment. Then, they should list any that are in exaltation and fall. As they do this, they should try to work with the ideas that those in exaltation have a special role to play in the unfolding of their potential and that any in fall represent the fading out of that planetary principle.

Planets in Houses

Focus

A planet expresses its energy in the house in which it is found. This is the same as saying that the presence of a planet will make the area of life represented by the house in which the planet is found, one of particular importance to the unfolding of the individuality.

In any natal chart, there will be houses without planets (untenanted), and others that may contain a number of planets.

This does not mean that the untenanted houses represent areas of life that will not feature in the life: The constant movement of the heavens ensures that in time some planets will move through all houses (see Endnote 1), but it does mean that developments in this area of life may have no special importance to the theme of the life. Conversely, a house that contains a number planets will be one of particular importance in the life, being the meeting place of different energies.

A planet will always be itself, assisted or hindered by the sign in which it is found, but the house placement will focus that energy.

For example, a person with Mars in Aries in the tenth house will direct his assertiveness into the building of his career, while a person with Mars in Aries in the second house will direct his energy into making and spending money. For the former, status and recognition would be the route to self-advancement; for the latter, the route would be through purchasing power, but the Aries influence would mean that both were highly determined and energetic in pursuit of their respective goals.

Angular placement

Planets that are close (within five degrees either side) to the hyleg points are particularly powerful.

- A luminary or planet in the first house, within five degrees of the ascendant, is deemed to be rising and will condition a person's appearance and the way he presents himself to the world.
- A luminary or planet in the tenth house, within five degrees of the MC, is described as culminating. It is very influential because it sheds its light over the entire chart. The chances are that a culminating planet will also be the most elevated planet (i.e. the planet closest to the MC. The only reason it would not be the most elevated planet would be if there were another planet, either side of the MC, that were closer still. One can have more than one culminating planet, but only one of them, obviously, can be the most

elevated. The most elevated planet, like the culminating planet, bathes the life in its light (see Endnote 2).

- A luminary or planet in the seventh house within five degrees of the descendant is described as setting, and early in the life at least, will indicate the kind of energy that a person will bring into his life through intimates - parents, guardians, siblings, friends and partners – in order to learn about using that energy. Later in life, he may be able to find this energy within himself.

- A luminary or planet in the fourth house within five degrees of the IC has no special name, but it describes the energy of the mother and the quality of the home life and gives a person a strong connection with the collective unconscious. Although such a planet does not have the strength of the other angular planets, it is nonetheless likely to be of significance in determining the quality of the life.

Astrological tradition states that the lives of people who are born with the Sun rising or setting may have lives of particular significance to others as the Sun casts the longest shadows at sunrise and sunset.

Planets adjacent to house cusps

Any planet that is one house but within five degrees of the cusp of the next house of a higher number is said to cast its influence in the next house rather than that in which it is situated. (The one exception to this ruling about houses of a higher number is that a planet in the twelfth house within five degrees of the ascendant would cast its light in the first house . In any case, such a planet would be identified as a rising planet.)

If we look at the example chart of Valentine (Part One *I* Chapter 2), we see that Valentine's Venus is in the first house but within five degrees of the second house (higher number). The influence of Venus, therefore, will be felt in the second house rather than the first. Similarly, his Saturn in the fourth house is within five degrees of the cusp of the fifth house (higher number). Its influence would be felt in that house rather than in the fourth house (see Endnote 3).

Students are advised to sort through the planets in their own charts and identify any planets that are:

- **Rising**
- **Culminating**
- **Setting**
- **Within five degrees (either side) of IC**
- **The most elevated planet in the chart**
- **Identify any planets whose the influence is working through the adjacent house**

Endnotes

1. The effects of time on the natal chart are covered in this author's book *Working with Time.*

2. The psychic Edgar Cayce claimed that the most elevated planet indicates the region of the solar system from which the child has come into incarnation. If this region of the solar system is taken to mean a plane of consciousness, then students may find some value in contemplating this idea.

3. In effect, these conditions are likely to mean that Valentine has a liking for good things, rather than having exceptionally good looks, which would be the case if Venus were working through the first house, and also create a difficult relationship with his father rather than his mother, which would be the case if the influence of Saturn were experienced through fourth house.

Chapter 10

Aspects

There are areas of astrology where the use of fewer words is better because this allows the principles to stand out. In the final analysis, it is a grasp of principles, not memorising other peoples' commentaries, that will create the confidence to work with astrology. Please resist the temptation to use astrological cookbooks, especially those dealing with aspects, because in such books, the principles get overlaid by a mass of detail and the student using them will actually lose confidence. I have seen this happened again and again. If you understand what each of the planets represents and the nature of the aspects, you can deduce what will be the effect when the two planets are in aspect. This is by far the better way to proceed.

✳✳✳

Figure 7 Aspects box: Valentine; February 14, 2000; 03:30; California, USA.

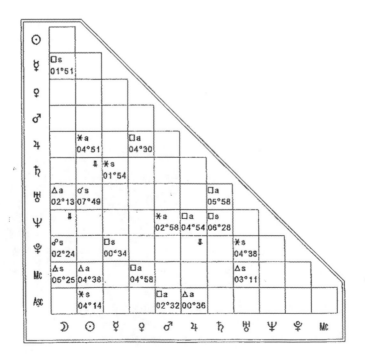

Aspects are defined as the angular relationship between planets. What this means is the shortest distance between to celestial bodies measured in degrees of the ecliptic, which, of course, is a circle.

- If, as is the case in Valentine's chart, the Sun is at Aquarius twenty-five, and Venus is at Capricorn twenty-five degrees, then the two bodies are thirty degrees apart and the aspect between them is a semisextile. The calculation of aspects is very easy once you get into the habit of remembering that:
- The signs always follow each other in the same order
- There are always thirty degrees in a sign
- Intercepted signs must be included in the count, which means that some houses could contain over 60 degrees. This will not be the case with the equal house system

Working with the Aspects

In this chapter, our concern is the nature of the aspects because the aspect between the planets will determine whether their relationship with each other is one of cooperation or frustration.

The aspects are a dialogue between the planets involved, and they provide the dynamics of the natal chart.

- Harmonious aspects create a situation of cooperation between planets.
- Stressful aspects create a situation of hostility or aggression between two planets with the slower interfering with the faster.
- There is a third, smaller category called neutral conjunctions in which two planets merely blend without the slower having any noticeable positive or detrimental effect on the other. In this case, the slower merely blends its nature with that of the faster.

In considering the effect of one planet upon another, it is important to remember the rule that the slower moving influences the faster moving.

- When they are in aspect, the Moon has no impact upon Pluto, but Pluto prevails upon the Moon with its qualities of destructiveness and intensity. When the aspect is harmonious, the Moon absorbs and works with these qualities. When the aspect is stressful, the Moon tries to repel Pluto, and the relationship between them and the houses with which they are involved is one of aggression.

Although we are focusing on just the ten most commonly used aspects, there are others that have their place in specialist branches of astrology.

Orbs of influence

Influence does not stop abruptly; rather, it fades out. The orb of influence is the number of degrees from exact that an aspect can be and still retain its power. There is no universally accepted standard for the orbs, and it is evident that American astrologers are inclined to use wider orbs than their British counterparts. This matter need not be made controversial. The point is that when recommended orbs are given, as they are below, they are guidelines to help students until they have enough experience to feel their own way.

Using the recommendations below:

- Two luminaries in aspect to each other will qualify for the maximum recommended orb given.
- Two planets in aspect to each other will qualify for the smallest recommended orb.
- A luminary and planet together would fall in the middle of the range.
- For example, using the table below:
- The Moon and Sun, in conjunction aspect with each other, have a maximum orb of ten degrees.
- Venus and Mars in conjunction aspect have a maximum orb of eight degrees.
- Venus and the Sun have a maximum orb of nine degrees.

Commonly Used Aspects

aspect	symbol	degrees	nature	status	maximum recommended orb of influence (degrees)
conjunction	☌	0'	variable-depending upon planets involved	major	8-10
semi-sextile	⚺	30	co-operative (H)	minor	3-5
semi-square	∠	45	provocative (S)	minor	3-5
sextile	⚹	60	supportive (H)	major	6-8
quintile	Q	72	creatively tense (H)	minor	3-5
square	□	90	aggressively interfering (S)	major	6-8
trine	△	120	constructive, flowing (H)	major	8-10
sesiquadrate	⚼	135	over-reactive (S)	minor	3-5
quincunx / injunct	⚻	150	disjunctive (S)	minor	3-5
opposition	☍	180	blocking (S)	major	8-10

Key:
H=harmonious
S= stressful

The major harmonious aspects are certain conjunctions (see table below):

- Sextile
- Trine

The major stressful aspects are certain conjunctions (see table below):
- Square
- Opposition

Although they are described as minor, the importance of the minor aspects given above should not be ·underestimated. The make a significant contribution to the workings of the mind.

The minor harmonions aspects are:
- Semi-sextile
- Quintile

The minor stressful aspects are:

- Semi-square
- Sesiquadrate
- Quincunx, also known as injunct

Although they are described as minor, the importance of the minor aspects given above should not be ·underestimated. The make a significant contribution to the workings of the mind.

Table of Conjunctions

Figure 8

	☉	☽	☿	♀	♂	♃	♄	⚷	♅	♆	♇
☉		H	N	H	S	H	S	S	S	H	S
☽			N	H	S	H	S	S	S	H	S
☿				H	S	H	S	S	S	S	S
♀					S	H	S	S	S	H	S
♂						H	S	S	S	S	S
♃							S	S	H	H	S
♄								S	S	S	S
⚷									N	S	S
♅										H	S
♆											H

Key:
H = harmonious
S = stressful

Aspects to the hylegs

In the language of esotericism, these points are said to 'cast no rays', and this has to be taken into consideration. The orbs of influence are significantly reduced.

- For all celestial bodies in conjunction aspect to the hylegs, use a maximum orb of influence of five degrees. As you will probably realize, this is the same concept as rising, setting, and culminating bodies.
- Theoretically, a point that casts no rays can receive only influences thrown from zero, ninety, and 180 degrees. In practice, this is not the case, and the major harmonious aspects should be considered in relation to the hylegs but with reduced orbs of influence. Those recommended are:

  - Sextile, maximum orb, two to four degrees

- Trine, maximum orb, three to five degrees

When examining the relationship between one celestial body and another, consider that:

- No celestial body will ever lose its essential nature, no matter how powerful the influence from another planet, but the slower planet will influence the faster moving planet by impressing upon it its own qualities.
- A fast moving body such as the Moon or Mercury may pick up many different influences, the relative strength of which will be determined by the closeness of the aspect and the slowness of the aspecting planet. The planet will express the influences it receives in the house in which it is located, and pass it into the houses which it rules.
- Each planet is located in a house, and each house represents an area of life, so when two planets are in aspect, the areas of life with which they are connected become involved too.
- The Sun may be the central organisor, but it is not the most powerful planet: The superior planets and the outer planets all influence the Sun.
- Two planets may be in different signs but still in conjunction aspect to each other.
- Be aware of the factors influencing planetary strength (e.g, angular placement, most elevated planet).

Students are advised to spend time with their own charts, working out the aspects between each planet before moving on to aspect configurations.

Aspect Configurations

Aspect configurations involve a number of planets in aspect to each other and collectively forming a pattern of significance.

There are a number of such patterns. In this lesson, we will focus upon the five most common:

- Stellium
- Bucket
- T-square
- Yod
- Grand cross

Such configurations are not rare, but neither will they be found in all charts. All configurations concentrate energy in a certain way for a specific effect.

There is, however, a configuration called a scatter pattern, which is a nonpattern, the planets being dotted all around the chart. This disperses the energy of the chart and makes it difficult for a person to focus and stick to a course of action.

In practice, aspect configurations dominate the chart, and the houses involved in the configuration represent areas of life that will be of particular importance. It is part of the astrologer's skill to be able to see how such a concentration of energy could assist an individual's development.

Please note that in all configurations described below, the standard orbs of influence are applicable.

Stellium

Definition:

Four or more planets all in conjunction aspect to each other, and to be technically accurate, all in the same sign.

In practice:

Three or more planets in conjunction aspect to each other in the same sign, and four planets in conjunction aspect to each other but involving two signs are still to be noted.

Effect:

Tremendous concentration of energy in one area of life, the outlet for which will be the fastest planet in the stellium.

Developmental purpose:

Compelling a person to function in an area of life that may have been an area of difficulty or prohibition in the past.

Figure 9

Stellium (in Aries in House 11)

- fastest moving planet Mercury, ruler of Ascendant and House 5
Koch House system ©Winstar Matrix software

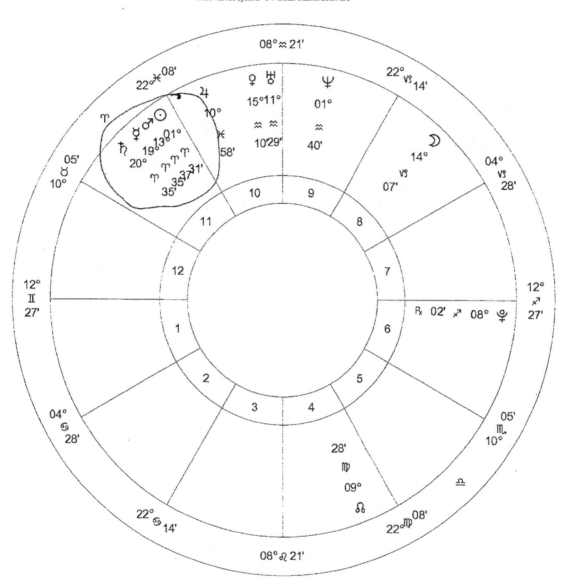

Bucket

Definition:

A concentration of planets in one half of the chart (contained within 180 degrees plus orbs)
- A single planet or a small cluster of planets in conjunction aspect to each other in the opposite half of the chart, creating the handle of the bucket.

Effect:

The planet or planets in the handle and the area of life involved will be the focal point of the chart and that energy principle/area of life will drive the life. When more than one planet comprises the handle, the fastest moving planet will provide the outlet for the others.

Developmental purpose:

Organising the life around one energy principle, the bucket is to be found in the charts of people who may have a specific task to fulfill on behalf of others in their lifetimes.

Figure 10

Bucket
- Handle: Jupiter retrograde in Taurus in House 12, ruler of Houses 8 & 11

Koch House system ©Winstar Matrix software

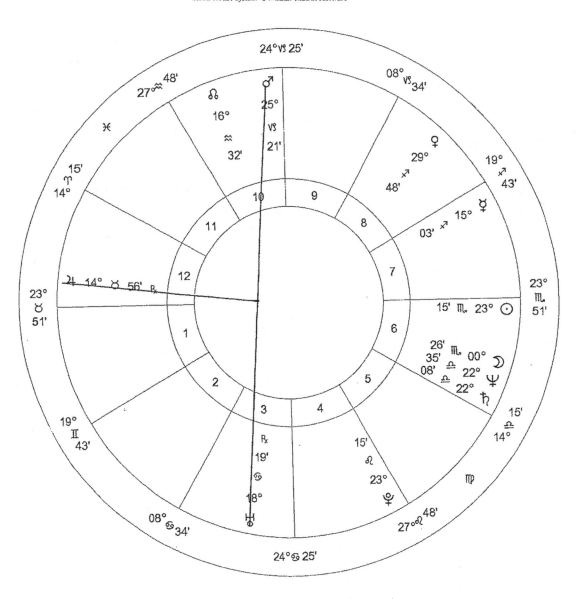

T-square

Definition:

Three or more planets in an aspectual arrangement involving one opposition and two squares with at least one planet common to both creating the stem of the T.

Effect:

The effect is to trap energy in the T figure, and this, being like a table with just three legs, creates an imbalance in the life until the person restores equilibrium by learning to operate in what is called the empty quarter (the house/area of life directly opposite the focal planet of the T-square).

Developmental purpose:

This arrangement is the way of encouraging development into the area of life that comprises the empty quarter. The encouragement is by means of hard lessons, and this configuration is found in the charts of people who understand the purpose of struggle and effort.

Figure 11

T square with conjunction of Saturn & Neptune as the focal planets
- fastest moving planet Saturn
- 'empty quarter' House 12

Koch House system ©Winstar Matrix software

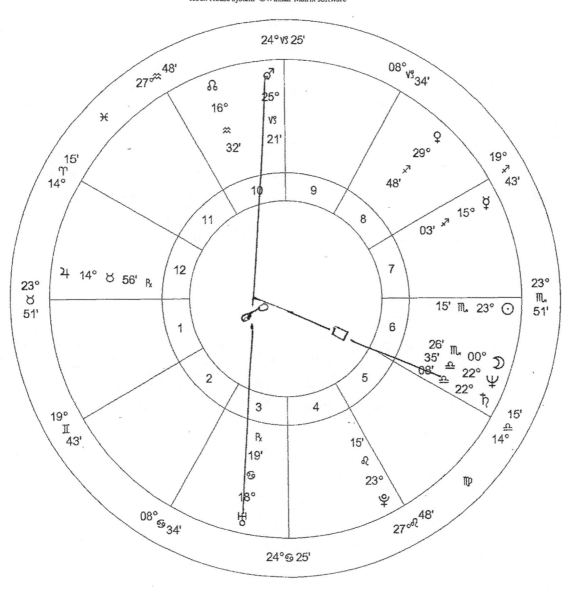

Yod

Definition:

Also called the finger of God or the finger of fate, the yod involves three or more planets making two quincunxes with at least one planet common to both (the focal planet),and one sextile.

In practice:

Look out for a variation on this in which a planet or planets are situated midway between the two planets making the sextile. This will create an opposition aspect with the focal planet and is called a tetrodic yod.

Effect:

The effect of this is to point at the focal planet and identify it as a planet that needs regenerating because it is operating in a dysfunctional way, the quincunx being the aspect of disjunction. This will start to happen once conscious effort enables the planets/houses involved in the sextile to cooperate with each other. As with all focal planets, if more than one is involved, the faster planet will provide the outlet.

Developmental purpose:

The yod singles out an energy principle for conscious reorientation, the implication being that it has been used or inadequately used in the past or has a special role to play in the lifetime. When the yod is tetrodic, the need to consciously regenerate the energy of the focal planet is intensified. The faster moving planet in the opposition will indicate the are of life which will provide a platform for the regenerated energy.

Figure 12

Yod with Mercury as the focal planet
- quincunxes from Jupiter in House 12& Uranus in House 3
  - sextile between Jupiter & Uranus

Koch House system ©Winstar Matrix software

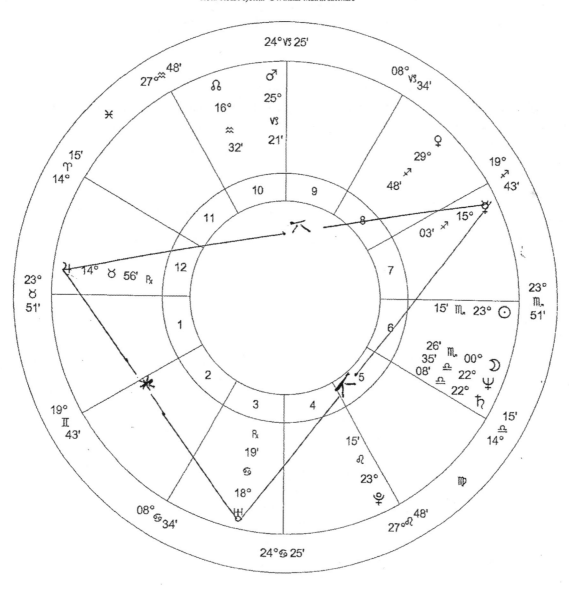

Grand cross

Definition: Four or more planets creating two oppositions and four squares.

Effect:

Esoterically, four is a very material number and implies limitations and restrictions. A person with a grand cross will go round in circles trying to find a way out from the frustration of being blocked by first one opposition and then the other. The modality of the cross will be of significance in understanding the self-defeating behaviour. A cardinal cross is violent and angry, while a fixed cross is mired in habit.

Unlike the T-square, the grand cross allows no empty quarter in which to move, although if one of the planets involved in the cross makes a major harmonious aspect to a planet not involved in the cross, this may be used as an escape route.

Developmental purpose:

This may be a purely karmic condition, representing the unavoidable result of cultivating certain attitudes over lifetimes.

Figure 13

Grand Cross

- opposition between the Moon & Sun, Houses 10 & 4 (Sun angular / most elevated planet)
- opposition between Saturn & Pluto House 1 (influence felt in House 2) & 7 (influence felt in House 8)
- square between the Sun & Pluto
- square between the Moon & Pluto
- share between the Moon & Saturn
- square between the Sun and Saturn
- Jupiter in House 8 (trine Moon and sextile Sun) is important to finding a way out of the Cross

Koch House system ©Winstar Matrix software

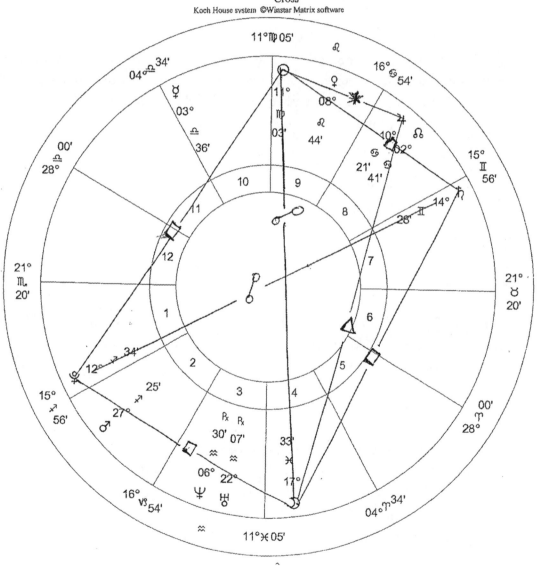

Chapter 11

More Advanced Considerations 1
Dispositors and Significators

Don't forget that astrology is a language and that an extensive vocabulary does not guarantee clarity of communication. No astrologer, no matter how proficient or practiced, will know all there is to know because the language is constantly evolving. Work well with what you understand, and don't be in too much of a hurry to add to it.

✳✳✳

Planets in Signs

Planetary dispositors

Any planet occupying a sign that is not its own disposits (or displaces) the planetary ruler of that sign and in doing so creates a link between itself and the desposited planets and the houses involved (see Endnote **1).**

Using Valentine's chart, it can be seen that:

- ☉ disposits ♅ (ruler of ♒) which is also in the second house.
- ☽ disposits ☿ (ruler of ♊) creating a link between third and sixth houses and between the eighth house of which the Moon is the ruler and the sixth and seventh houses that Mercury rules.

This can be done for all planets to uncover how it and the house in which it is placed and which it rules interact with others.

Sole dipositor

This is an unusual condition creating a chain of dispositing situations that link a succession of planets and houses.

An example of this would be ☽ in ♊ dispositing ☿ in ♈ dispositing ♂ in ♐ dispositing ♃ in ♑.

Mutual reception

This occurs when a planet disposits a planet which is then found in the sign of its dispositor. This situation will be found and creates a flowing relationship between the planets and the houses involved.

In Valentine's chart, an example of this is

♀ in ♑ dispositing ♄ which is to be found in ♉ the sign ruled by ♀

Planets in Houses

Planetary rulerships

Every planet rules a house naturally and accidentally.

A natural ruler governs the sign to which a house corresponds; therefore:

♂ is the natural ruler of **House 1**
♀ is the natural ruler of **House 2**
☿ is the natural ruler of **House 3**
☽ is the natural ruler of **House 4**
☉ is the natural ruler of **House 5**
☿ is the natural ruler of **House 6**
♀ is the natural ruler of **House 7**
♂/♀ are the natural rulers of **House 8**
♃ is the natural ruler of **House 9**
♄ is the natural ruler of **House 10**
♄/♅ are the natural rulers of **House 11**
♃/♆ are the natural rulers of **House 12**

Natural rulerships are unchanging, and each natural ruler represents the area of life/house it governs. Thus, Jupiter is the natural representative of all things pertaining to the ninth house.

Accidental rulers, however, are determined by the signs on the cusps of the houses in any given natal chart (see Endnote 3).

- With reference to Valentine's chart, it can be seen that:

♃ is the accidental ruler of **House 1 & 12**
♄ is the accidental ruler of **House 2**
♃/♆ are the accidental rulers of **House 1**
♂ is the accidental ruler of **House 4**
♀ is the accidental ruler of **House 5**
☿ is the accidental ruler of **Houses 6 & 7**
☽ is the accidental ruler of **House 8**
☿ is the accidental ruler of **House 9**
♀ is the accidental ruler of **House 10**
♂ is the accidental ruler of **House 11**

- Houses that share an accidental ruler will be linked in the life of that person in a very direct way. In Valentine's case, for example, the first, third, and twelfth houses and the things governed by these houses will be linked together, and all three houses will be linked to the ninth house because Jupiter is the natural ruler of the ninth house. As will be seen, these links are of the greatest importance in chart interpretation because they form the structure of the mind.

Significators

The accidental ruler of a house is called a significator. This is the same idea as the representative mentioned above but with more specific applicability. Each planet is a significator of an area of life, and each significator is to be found somewhere in the natal chart, giving emphasis to one area of life. This fact creates further links of importance.

In Valentine's case, Saturn is the significator of money and values. Through the fact that Saturn's influence is felt through the fifth house, money and values are directly linked with creative expression and individuality. Mercury is the significator of his relationships, as well as the significator of overseas travel and spiritual questing (the ninth house), and these create a link between these two areas of life.

For practical purposes, it is very important to understand the role of significators and dispositors. The astrologer's skill consists very largely of spotting and interpreting the connections made between them in a chart. Advancing this process will be our concern in the final chapters of this book.

For now, using their own charts, students are advised to check out the dispositors and mutual receptions and identify which planet in the chart is the significator or relationships (the ruler of the seventh house) and career (the ruler of the tenth house), as well as whether there are any planets in the seventh or tenth house, and if so, which houses they rule.

Endnotes

1. It is the depth of the practitioner's knowledge of disposition that makes Hindu astrology as formidably precise as it is. In the West, we handle this concept in a very basic way: We acknowledge the connection created between two houses (areas of life) by this process, but we do not focus on the permutations at the level of form created by this interchange. A Hindu astrologer learns the permutations created by two luminaries, five planets, and twelve houses, much as we learn the alphabet or a multiplication table.

2. Owing to changing literary styles, some of the terms used in astrology convey very little to the contemporary reader. In this context, accidental means dependent upon the time of birth.

Chapter 12

More Advanced Considerations 2

Planetary Representations

For as long as we are working with and thinking about astrology, we will be adding to our understanding of the significance of our tools. And as our understanding expands, so our appreciation of them will increase.

✲✲✲

In this chapter, we are deepening our understanding of the planets by looking at their significance in an esoterically oriented approach to horoscopical interpretation (Endnote 1). Firstly, let us remind ourselves of which house rules naturally.

Celestial Body	Symbol	Ruler of House
Sun	☉	5
Moon	☽	4
Mercury	☿	3 & 6
Venus	♀	2 & 7
Mars	♂	1(&8)
Jupiter	♃	9 (&12)
Saturn	♄	10 (&11)
Chiron	⚷	Connected to Houses 6&9
Uranus	♅	11
Neptune	♆	12
Pluto	♀ / ♇	8

Sun: The principle of life and consciousness

⊙

- Rules the sign Leo
- In detriment in the sign Aquarius
- Elevated in the sign Aries
- Falls in the sign Libra

- Natural ruler of the fifth house and significator of all things ruled by that house
- Accidental ruler of the house in the horoscope that has the sign Leo on its cusp and the personalised significator of the things ruled by that house

The Sun is a star, not a planet. It is the representative of a higher order than the planets and in the horoscope should be understood to stand for the egoic body, or the soul's representative, on the mental plane. The egoic (or causal) body forms when we get out physical bodies under control and use energy more efficiently, and develops as our sense of individuality opens out new experiences to us.

The Sun represents our identity or who we understand ourselves to be. Strengthening that sense of identity is the prime requirement of the lifetime. This means expressing the qualities of the sign and being active in the area of life in which the Sun is found and consciously linking in those areas of life indicated by the house that the Sun rules accidentally. This brings the experiences which will develop the egoic body in accordance with the design of the lifetime, and strengthen the sense of individuality.

Encouraged in this by the perspectives of popular astrology, we tend to think we are born expressing our Sun signs. This is not the case. We have to learn to express them during the course of our lifetimes. This can be done with more or less consciousness. A conscious expression will have more definition, effectiveness and authenticity.

The Sun is the natural ruler of the fifth house, so its expression in a horoscope will always imply awareness of individuality and creative capacity, qualities that, traditionally, the father is considered to encourage.

For this reason, aspects to the Sun describe the experiences with the father around the issue of developing and expressing identity.

- The Sun influences the Moon, Mercury, and Venus.
- It is influenced by Mars, Jupiter, Saturn, Chiron, Uranus, Neptune, and Pluto.

In esoteric astrology, the Sun transmits the second ray of love: wisdom.

Moon: The principle of continuity

)

- Rules the sign Cancer
- In detriment in the sign Capricorn
- Elevated in the sign Taurus
- Falls in the sign Scorpio

- Natural ruler of the fourth house and significator of all things ruled by that house
- Accidental ruler of the house in the horoscope that has the sign Cancer on its cusp and the personalised significator of the things ruled by that house.

The Moon is a satellite of Earth, and the relationship between the two is one of mutual dependency since, energetically, it is fed by all that dies on Earth. In turn, it regulates organic life on Earth through which life takes form.

In a horoscope, the Moon represents the past (forms, identities, experiences) that are recorded in our psyche and expressed through our emotional natures.

The Moon also represents the mother, the function of whom is to perpetuate and provide continuity and the home that is the place of shelter for the form.

For this reason, aspects to the Moon describe the experiences with the mother around the issue of receiving nurturing.

The Moon is the natural ruler of the fourth house, so its expression in a horoscope will always imply the conditioning effect of the past from the family, the culture of birth, and racial heritage.

- The Moon influences no other body in the heavens, but it is influenced by them all. In esoteric astrology, the Moon attracts the fourth ray of harmony through conflict. Esoteric astrology recognises that the Moon represents those things from which we must move on in the interests of progress, but with which we must also make our peace because they are part of our evolution.

Esoterically, the Moon is said to rule the physical body.

Mercury: The principle of communication

☿

- Rules the signs Gemini and Virgo
- In detriment in the sign Sagittarius
- Elevated in the sign Virgo
- Falls in the sign Pisces

- Natural ruler of the third and sixth houses and
significator of all things ruled by those houses
- Accidental ruler of the house in the horoscope that has the signs Gemini and Virgo
on its cusp and the personalised significator of the things ruled by that house

Mercury will never be far away from the Sun . In fact, it will never be more than twenty-eight degrees and can therefore make no major stressful aspect to the Sun .

Mercury communicates between the level of the Sun and that of the planets. As such, it is the symbol of duality but also of the possibility of fusion. Mercury makes us aware of self and others, lower and higher, and analysis and synthesis.

The house position of Mercury in a horoscope indicates the area through which we will come by soul awareness. This may be a different house from that in which the Sun is positioned.

In a horoscope, Mercury rules human speech and hearing, education, and all systems of communication.

Mercury will always be the natural ruler of the third and sixth houses, so its expression will always imply interaction, exchange, and service.

- Mercury influences the Moon.
- It is influenced by Venus, Mars, Jupiter, Saturn, Chiron, Uranus, Neptune, and Pluto.

In esoteric astrology, Mercury transmits the fourth ray of harmony through conflict. *Note: When Mercury is in conjunction aspect to the Sun (a condition known as combust), its ability to create awareness of duality is impaired: The Sun, representing the identity, dominates, and a person tends to be very locked into his own way of looking at life and unresponsive to the realities of others.*

Venus: The principle of attraction
♀
- Rules Taurus and Libra
- In detriment in Scorpio
- Elevated in Pisces
- Falls in Virgo

- Natural ruler of the second and seventh houses and
significator of all things ruled by those houses
- Accidental ruler of the house in the horoscope that has the signs Taurus and Libra
on its cusp and the personalised significator of the things ruled by that house

Venus, like Mercury, will never be far away from the Sun . In fact, it will never be more than sixty degrees and can therefore make no major stressful aspect to the Sun .

The house in which Venus is found indicates the area of life in which a person will meet what attracts them and what they value. This includes people, possessions, and activities of a kind that accords with the house in which it is found.

In a horoscope, Venus rules order, affinities, beauty, and harmony.

Venus will always be the natural ruler of the second and seventh houses, so its expression will always imply an awareness of relationship, whether that is to things or people.

- Venus influences the Moon and Mercury.
- It is influenced by Mars, Jupiter, Saturn, Chiron, Uranus, Neptune, and Pluto.

In esoteric astrology, Venus transmits the fifth ray of concrete science.

Esoterically, Venus is said to be Earth's older, more spiritually evolved sister.

Mars: The principle of assertion
♂
- Rules Aries and Scorpio
- In detriment in Libra
- Elevated in Capricorn
- Falls in Cancer

- Natural ruler of the first and eighth houses and significator of all things ruled by those houses
- Accidental ruler of the house in the horoscope that has the signs Aries and Scorpio on its cusp and the personalised significator of the things ruled by that house

Mars' orbit allows it to make all the major aspects, both harmonious and stressful, to the Sun .

The house in which Mars is found indicates the area of life in which a person will expend energy in pursuit of what he considers worthwhile. For this reason, it is often used as a key to the kind of work that a person will find fulfilling.

In a horoscope, Mars rules drive, passion, and conflict.

Mars will always be the natural ruler of the first and eighth houses, so its expression will always involve assertiveness. In the first house, Mars is naturally energetic and assertive; in the eighth house, Mars is fearful of the consequences of assertiveness and aggression.

- Mars influences the Moon, Mercury, Venus, and the Sun .
- It is influenced by Jupiter, Saturn, Chiron, Uranus, Neptune, and Pluto.

In esoteric astrology, Mars transmits the sixth ray of will to power.

Esoterically, Mars is said to rule the emotional body.

Jupiter: The principle of expansion
♃

- Rules Sagittarius and Pisces
  - In detriment in Virgo
  - Elevated in Cancer
  - Falls in Capricorn

- Natural ruler of the ninth and twelfth houses and significator of all things ruled by those houses
- Accidental ruler of the house in the horoscope that has the signs Sagittarius and Pisces on its cusp and the personalised significator of the things ruled by that house

Jupiter's orbit allows it to make all the major aspects, both harmonious and stressful to the Sun .

In a horoscope, Jupiter rules exploration and questing and all spiritual, religious, and philosophical systems that encourage human development.

The house in which Jupiter is found indicates the area of life in which a person will feel least restricted. For this reason, it is often used as a key to the kind of activities that will move us on from routine and habituality. It is also known as the Great Benefic. A prominant or badly aspected Jupiter in a natal chart can be the cause of over-indulgence and licentiousness.

Jupiter will always be the natural ruler of the ninth and twelfth, so its expression will always involve a search for the broader view that is inclusive and ends separation and limitation.

- Jupiter influences the Moon, Mercury, Venus, the Sun, and Mars.
- It is influenced by Saturn, Chiron, Uranus, Neptune, and Pluto.

In esoteric astrology, Jupiter transmits the second ray of love: wisdom.

Esoterically, Jupiter rules the higher emotional body.

Saturn: The principle of restriction
ħ

- Rules Capricorn and Aquarius
  - In detriment in Cancer
    - Elevated in Libra
      - Falls in Aries

- Natural ruler of the tenth and eleventh houses and significator of all things ruled by those houses
- Accidental ruler of the house in the horoscope that has the signs Capricorn and Aquarius on its cusp and the personalised significator of the things ruled by that house

Saturn's orbit allows it to make all the major aspects, both harmonious and stressful, to the Sun .

The house in which Saturn is found indicates the area of life in which a person will encounter difficulties and limitations. It is, therefore, the area of life in which we have to apply ourselves with as much consciousness as possible to overcome the restrictions. If we do this, we will learn from experience and eventually come to understand the problems created by our assumptions about life (an inherited mentality) and our conditioned way of dealing with things.

In a horoscope, Saturn rules the father and authority figures, discipline, experience, structures, and all arrangements that provide structure and organisation.

Saturn will always be the natural ruler of the tenth and eleventh houses, so its expression will always involve creating structures that will protect and give strength to the isolated individual. Although Saturn is traditionally associated with the father, it will be the most authoritative parent who will externalise this principle in an individual's life.

- Saturn influences the Moon, Mercury, Venus, the Sun, Mars, and Jupiter.
- It is influenced by Saturn, Chiron, Uranus, Neptune, and Pluto.
- In esoteric astrology, Saturn transmits the third ray of knowledge.

Esoterically, Saturn is said to rule the mental body.

Chiron: The principle of redemption
⚷

- Rules Virgo and Sagittarius
- Natural ruler of the sixth and ninth houses and significator of all things ruled by those houses

Chiron's orbit allows it to make all the major aspects, both harmonious and stressful, to the Sun .

The house in which Chiron is found indicates the area of life in which a person will encounter spiritually challenging situations that will cause him trauma until he learns how to deal with Chironic energy, which requires him to abandon his separatist stand and begin to share as much as he understands with others. Then his own hurts will both heal and enable him to be of help to others. It is, therefore, the area of life in which a person has to learn to share such understanding as he has. In Greek mythology, Chiron is the wounded healer.

- Chiron influences the Moon, Mercury, Venus, the Sun, Mars, Jupiter, and Saturn.
- It is influenced by Uranus, Neptune, and Pluto.

In esoteric astrology, Chiron transmits the fourth ray of harmony through conflict.

Although Chiron is still finding its way into the astrologer's tool kit, it is an important planet for any astrologer who is using his craft to give spiritual guidance. Chiron has been called the scar on the soul, but the house in which it is found indicates an area of life that will become a place of accomplishment. Potentially, it will become a place of strength, because it is an area of life in which we are growing in spiritual maturity.

Uranus: The principle of liberation
⛢

- Rules Aquarius

- Natural ruler of the eleventh house and significator of all things ruled by this house
  - Accidental ruler of the house in the horoscope that has the sign Aquarius on its cusp, and the personalised significator of the things ruled by that house

Uranus' orbit allows it to make all the major aspects, both harmonious and stressful, to the Sun .

The house in which Uranus is found indicates the area of life in which a person will encounter unexpected and sometimes traumatic events, frequently involving separation. The purpose of these developments is to free a person from attachments that have now served their purpose. Uranus is the custodian of development.

In a horoscope, Uranus rules the intuition, electricity, the unexpected, the unusual, and the alternative. It represents the occult way rather than the mystical way.

Uranus is the natural ruler of the eleventh house, so its expression will always involve a relinquishing of established attitudes and practices that isolate and restrict. Uranus rules the disciplines of astrology and yoga and all systems that connect above and below.

- Uranus influences the Moon, Mercury, Venus, the Sun, Mars, Jupiter, Saturn, and Chiron.
- It is influenced by Neptune and Pluto.

In esoteric astrology, Uranus transmits the seventh ray of ceremonial order.

Neptune: The principle of absorption
♆

- Rules Pisces

- Natural ruler of the twelfth house and significator of all things ruled by this house
- Accidental ruler of the house in the horoscope that has the sign Pisces on its cusp and the personalised significator of the things ruled by that house

Neptune's orbit allows it to make all the major aspects, both harmonious and stressful, to the Sun .

The house in which Neptune is found indicates the area of life in which we will encounter the ideas, practices, and experiences that will inspire us and give us the sense of being part of something greater than ourselves. In that area of life, a person will be capable of selfless behaviour but also confusion as to boundaries and entitlements.

In a horoscope, Neptune rules the mystical sense, psychism, clairvoyance, and anaesthesia. A prominent Neptune will make a person psychically sensitive. When it makes stressful aspects to inner planets, it can produce addictions to drugs, drink, and other forms of escapism. Neptune represents mysticism, emotionally based forms of spirituality, and self-sacrifice.

Neptune is the natural ruler of the twelfth house, so its expression will always involve a sense of being part of something higher and more purposeful than everyday life.

- Neptune influences the Moon, Mercury, Venus, the Sun, Mars, Jupiter, Saturn, Chiron, and Uranus.
- It is influenced by Pluto.

In esoteric astrology, Neptune transmits the sixth ray of devotion.

Pluto: The principle of transformation

- Rules Scorpio
- Natural ruler of the eighth house and significator of all things ruled by this house
- Accidental ruler of the house in the horoscope that has the sign Scorpio on its cusp and the personalised significator of the things ruled by that house

Pluto's orbit allows it to make all the major aspects, both harmonious and stressful, to the Sun.

Pluto changes consciousness. The house in which Pluto is found indicates the area of life in which we will encounter the people, ideas, practices, and experiences that will bring about a change in our understanding of that aspect of life. The process involves ridding the emotional nature of hidden desires and attachments by driving them out into the open. At this time, Pluto, which was unknown to our grandparents, is the most potent planetary agent of transformation.

In a horoscope, Pluto rules death on all levels (mental, emotional, and physical), sex, power, criminality, and the taboo. A prominent Pluto will attract profound, sometimes shocking experiences and make a person an agent for transformative energy that frequently expresses itself through a gift for healing.

Pluto is the natural ruler of the eighth house, and its expression will always involve emotionality and intensity.

- Pluto influences all the other bodies in the solar system.
- It is itself influenced by none.

In esoteric astrology, Pluto transmits the first ray of will to power.

Endnote

1. These ideas, including the concept of the seven rays, are given fuller treatment in *Transitional Astrology*.

Chapter 13

More Advanced Considerations 3

The Lunar Nodes and Part of Fortune

When one has developed a certain competence, one of the pleasures of astrology is to experiment with techniques and features drawn from the widening pool of nonbasic data. These include declinations, the asteroids, midpoints, critical degrees, and Arabic parts, to mention just a few. It is not appropriate to voice an opinion on the value of these things because their value is derived entirely from their usefulness to individual astrologers and to their particular ways of working. This is why each astrologer should experiment to find his or her rightful level and approach. There are many books written on these more specialised aspects of horoscopy, although finding them may take an Internet search rather than a trip to your local bookstore.

***

In this section, we are looking at two features of the natal chart that are not themselves planets but interact with the planetary world. They are included in most chart construction software, and if they are not, they are not difficult to ascertain. The lunar nodes may be taken straight from an ephemeris, and the part of fortune requires a short calculation that, of itself, offers valuable food for thought.

The value of both these features is enhanced by the consideration that they identify planets of special importance to the development of the individual: the planet (or luminary) disposited by the north node and that disposited by the part of fortune.

The Lunar Nodes

Astronomically, the nodes are the point on the ecliptic that the orbiting Moon crosses on its way into the northern celestial hemisphere (north node) and then on its way back into the Southern hemisphere (south node).

- Because it is astrological protocol, all ephemerides give the north node, although this may not be stated. The south node has to be found by polarity. The degree will be the same in both cases, and the signs will be opposites (eg, north node Taurus eighteen degrees; south node Scorpio eighteen degrees).
- Some ephemerides and software give the true node (i.e. exact placement), others give the mean node based upon the Moon's average daily motion. The difference between the two is not going to be more than one degree, and whether the true node is to be preferred over the mean node is something that astrologers should decide for themselves, if they have reason to believe it is a matter of significance.

Symbol:

℥ North node: heading upward
℥ South node: heading downward

The symbols for the nodes, especially that of the north node, is very similar to that of the glyph for the sign Leo. The difference is that both curled ends are closed. This similarity is not without significance to the esoterically minded astrologer. Under the sign Leo, we become aware of our individuality, and this represents the highest point of development for the human personality. The subsequent reabsorption and spiritualisation of the isolated individual is considered to be a stage of development that belongs to soul consciousness, rather than personality experience.

North Node ℥	South Node ℥	Learning experience
Aries	Libra	Assertiveness and how to be personally effective
Taurus	Scorpio	Groundedness and e motional control
Gemini	Sagittarius	Intellectual perspectives and detachment
Cancer	Capricorn	Emotional sensitivity and feminine perspectives
Leo	Aquarius	Individ uality and creative
Virgo	Pisces	potency: Authenticity Focus and precision
Libra	Aries	Awareness of others and balance
Scorpio	Taurus	Emotional maturity; insightfulness
Sagittarius	Gemini	Spiritual responsiveness
Capricorn	Cancer	Material responsibility and self-sufficiency
Aquarius	Leo	Group values and planetary responsibility
Pisces	Virgo	Compassion and a sense of the unity underlying life's variety

The north node indicates the quality of consciousness we are trying to unfold. To express the north node, placement will take effort and awareness. The south node indicates the kind of experiences that have been formative of consciousness in development to date. The sign and house position of the south node describe a way of being that is very familiar and that we are likely to express instinctively.

Both nodes disposit planets that will give certain houses (areas of life) special importance in the unfolding of a life. The influence coming from that disposited by the north node will be progressive, while that disposited by the south node will draw us into the past.

The state of affairs in consciousness indicated by the lunar nodes is the backdrop against which the detail of the life of the life must be placed. It may be likened to the slow-moving hand of a clock.

The Part of Fortune (or Fortuna)

The part of fortune owes nothing to astronomy. It is not a point in space, but rather, the most widely known of the ratios known as the Arabic parts.

There are books written on the Arabic parts, and some software includes them, complete with details on how they are deduced.

They are fun to experiment with, although an astrologer realises very early on that his problem is not how to find out more information but rather how to manage that which he has. For this reason, the innumerable Arabic parts tend to fall under the heading of too much information.

The part of fortune, however, has always enjoyed special status, and in older astrology texts, it is sometimes called Fortuna.

- Symbol: ⊗

Astrological significance

The symbol for the part of fortune is very similar to that of planet Earth (i.e. the cross of matter within the circle of spirit). Again, this similarity is not coincidental. In the chart, the part of fortune indicates attachment. The house sign and house position of Fortuna indicates an area of fascination, even obsession.

In orthodox astrology, the part of fortune has been reduced to a significator of wealth and possession, the inference being that this is what interests more people most. Consequently, it has been under used and, to some degree, trivialized.

The house position of Fortuna indicates the area of life that exerts a great fascination for the personality in incarnation. This fascination may operate in a subliminal way and may not be consciously acknowledged by us, or we may be so identified with it that, like the ground we are standing upon, we cannot see it because our feet are covering it.

Esotericism teaches us that it is desire that pulls us back into incarnation, drawn like fishes on a line, out of the sea onto dry land. If that kind of desire is what fortune describes, and it may well, then we need to acknowledge it and work with it as consciously as possible (Endnote 1).

The planet disposited by Fortuna, and the house in which it is found, will add to our understanding of the nature of this powerful desire and to the way that it is working out in everyday life.

Calculating the Part of Fortune

The part of fortune is a ratio.

It is calculated from the sum of the longitude of the ascendant, plus the longitude of the Moon minus the longitude of the Sun .

For the purposes of this calculation, each sign is given a numerical value. These values are derived from the thirty-degree share of the circle occupied by each sign (12 x 30 = 360 degrees)

Aries 0
Taurus 1
Gemini 2
Cancer 3
Leo 4
Virgo 5
Libra 6
Scorpio 7
Sagittarius 8
Capricorn 9
Aquarius 10
Pisces 11

Remember that there are:

- **Sixty minutes in a degree**
- **Thirty degrees in a sign**
- **Twelve signs in the zodiacal circle**

Thus, if the longitude of
- The Moon is Libra sixteen degrees, twenty minutes
- The ascendant is Gemini fifteen degrees, thirty-five minutes
- The Sun Pisces is fifteen degrees six minutes

The sum will be laid out as follows:

```
Moon  6   16   20
Asc.  2   15   35 +
      9   01   55
Sun  11   15   06 -
     10   16   49
```

Part of fortune = Aquarius sixteen degrees, forty-nine minutes

Endnote

1. In *Autobiography of a Yogi*, Paramahansa Yogananda tells the story of the devotee kept in incarnation by one remaining wish. That wish was to see again his teacher whom he had known in a .past life. When at last he did meet with him, the devotee died on the spot. Take that story on whatever level you like. Those who of us who wish to get the hooks out of ourselves need to understand the part of fortune.

Part Four

Interpretation

Chapter 14

Prioritising Information

Looking at the completed natal chart in a state of near despair because one has not a clue what it means is an experience that every astrology student has to go through. And it can be something of trauma. This is the point at which many give up astrology altogether. Many more still do something rather more oblique: They abandon the idea of ever penetrating a chart for themselves, and although they remain very interested in the language of astrology, they fall back upon reading other people's interpretations of the planets, houses, and signs and never attempt a synthesis, which is what chart interpretation amounts to. The basic problem is lack of confidence. Chart interpretation is not anything that one can approach diffidently. Make the chart speak to you. The way to do this is to put questions to it. Questions have brought the language of astrology into being, and questions will bring an individual chart to life. Even after all these years of astrological practice, I do not look at a chart, and 'see it all' (whatever that might be) at a glance: I am, rather, collecting valuable information in preparation for formulating the questions I will put to it, and that will tell me what I need to know.

∗∗∗

It is a great liberation when we no longer feel the need to prepare a reading against a pre-existing checklist of considerations. Confident in the knowledge that we will know where to look to find the information that we need, we can stop worrying about ourselves and how well rehearsed we are, and give our full attention to the questions put to us. But until then, it is helpful to follow a system that enables us to order information from the natal chart, so that we can prepare what we want to say in advance.

Prioritising information is a useful exercise. It focuses the mind and can bring out unexpected factors. Looking at Valentine's chart, it is not immediately obvious that Pluto is the most significant planet in it, but as will be shown, this proves to be the case.

Prioritising information about the signs

Although it should be obvious from looking at the chart, which are the most strongly represented signs, it is no bad thing to collect this information together systematically.

Collecting this information helps to establish the temperament.

A weighting method is recommended:

Award points:

- Three points for each luminary
- Three points for Saturn
- Three points to the sign on the ascendant and the MC
- Two points to the signs occupying the other hylegs
- Three points to the sign containing the ruling planet
- Two points to a sign containing its planetary ruler
- Three points to the sign containing the north node
- Two points to the sign containing the south node
- Two points to the sign containing the part of fortune
- Two points to the sign that contains the most elevated planet, even if this is the same as a planet on the MC
- Two points to any sign containing a stationary planet (Endnote 1)
- Two points to every planet contained within a stellium
- Two points to the focal planet of yod or T-square
- One point for every planet within each sign, regardless of whether it has been counted in any of the above categories

Tally the points

- Note the element and quality that scores the highest number of points.
- Note the number of points scored by the other elements and qualities, and ascertain whether there is any element, quality, or modality that is not represented or scores a very low count. A deficiency will cause imbalance.
- Consider the relationship of this sign to that on the ascendant. Is there conflict between them or are they compatible? They may be one and the same, of course.

Let us do this exercise with reference to the chart of Valentine.

sign of ♇	♈	♉	♊	♋	♌	♍	♎	♏	♐	♑	♒	♓
☉											3	
☽			3									
♄		3										
Asc.+ M.C							3		3			
ruling planet	3											
own planet	2											
other hylegs	2		2									
☊					3							
☋											2	
⊗	2											
most elevated planet									2			
staty. planet												
stellium												
focal planets of T squares & yods												2
any planet	2	1	1						2	1	3	1
Total	**11**	**4**	**6**	**0**	**3**	**0**	**3**	**0**	**7**	**1**	**10**	**3**

Distribution over the Elements:

Fire	Air	Earth	Water
21	19	5	3

Distribution over the Qualities:

Cardinal	Fixed	Mutable
15	17	16

Distribution: Masculine/Feminine:

Masculine	Feminine
40	8

Ascendant sign: Sagittarius: Fire
Dominant sign: Aries: Fire

The analysis based on sign reveals the following key features:

- The dominant sign is Aries (fire), although Aquarius (air), which is the Sun sign, is also strong. The blend of fire and air produces energy, enthusiasm, and inspiration.
- The dominant sign that also contains the ruling planet and the rising sign are fire signs. This means that the way that Valentine presents himself to the world will not counteract the energy that is so dominant in his personality. This will permit effective expression. The elements of water and more especially earth are seriously underrepresented, however. A lack of water makes a person unsympathetic and unimaginative. A lack of earth inclines a person toward ineffectiveness and impracticality, which, in turn, tends to be the cause of frustration and underachievement. This imbalance is likely to prove to be of crucial importance in the unfolding of his life.
- The qualities are well-balanced, which will permit an experimental and initiating approach to life tempered by tenacity.
- With the masculine signs dominating so thoroughly, there is going to be a selfish, gung-ho quality to this life that will surely produce relationship difficulties. This is tempered to some degree by the Moon in Libra in the sixth house.

As we progress with the interpretation, we hope to be able to see the developmental purpose served by this masculine imbalance.

Prioritising information about the planets

Disciplines to remember: The orbs of influence

Award:

- Three points to the ruling planet
- Three points to rising planet and planet on the descendant
- Three points to a planet on MC and planet on IC
- Three points to most elevated planet
- Three points to a planet in its sign*I*exaltation
- One point to a planet in its detriment*I*fall
- Three points a planet in its own house
- Three points to stationary planets
- Three points to any unaspected planet
- Three points to focal planets of yods and T-squares
- Two points to all the other planets involved in the yod or T-square

- Three points the fastest moving planet in a stellium
- Two points to all other planets involved in the stellium
- Two points to all planets involved in a grand trine and grand cross
- Three points to the two planets involved in the closest stressful aspect
- Two point to all planets involved in major stressful aspects (conjunctions, squares, quincunxes, and oppositions)
- Three points to the two planets involved in the closest harmonious aspect
- One point to all planets involved in major harmonious aspects (sextiles and trines), excluding
- most harmonious (noted previously)
- Three points to the planet involved in the creation of the most aspects

Tally the points

Using the chart of Valentine

Planet	☉	☽	☿	♀	♂	♃	♄	⚷	♅	♆	♇
Ruling planet						3					
Rising planet / planet on desc.											
Planet on MC/IC											
Most elevated planet											3
Planet in own sign/exhaltation					3			3			
Planet in own house			3	3							
Planet in fall/detriment	1		1								
Staty. planet											
Unaspected planet											
Tsquares / yods:focal planets			3								
Tsquares/yods: other planets		2						2			2
Stelliums:fastest moving planet											
Stelliums: other planets											
Grand cross / trine											
Closest stressful aspect			3								3
major stressful	2	2+2		2		2+2	2	2+2	2	2	2+2+2
Closest harmonious		3							3		
Major harmonious	1		1		1	1	1		1	1	1
Most aspects											3
Total	**4**	**9**	**11**	**5**	**4**	**8**	**3**	**6**	**9**	**3**	**18**

The most significant planet is Pluto situated in the twelfth house, accidental ruler of the eleventh house and natural ruler of the eighth house.

The other planet of major significance is Mercury.
Remembering disciplines, we know that the slowest moving planet is the most powerful.

This analysis reveals that:

- Pluto is not only the most powerful planet in Valentine's chart, but it is also the most significant. This will make it a tremendous force in his energy pattern, but because it is coming out of the twelfth house, it is likely to be experienced as coming from outside himself, a force beyond his control. This placement of Pluto brings aggression, both physical and emotional, into a person's life, starting in childhood. But its rewards are psychic awareness, and exceptional powers of creative visualisation.
- The closest stressful aspect is the square between Mercury and Pluto. The impact of this aspect will be felt in the third house, as well as in the sixth and ninth houses, of which Mercury is the ruler. The indications are that aggression experienced in childhood will colour both Valentine's personal reality and his capacity to communicate, which are both third house matters. Mercury in Pisces is Mercury in its fall that expresses itself verbally as a muddled and imprecise but psychically is very sensitive and aware. The closest harmonious aspect is between Saturn and Mercury. Again, the impact of this aspect will be felt in the third house, and to some degree, this will provide stability and counteract the disrupting influence of Pluto upon communication.

Prioritising information about the houses

Again, as with the signs, simply looking at a chart reveals the emphasis, but it may be usefully subject to a more careful analysis

Collecting this information discloses the areas of life through which a person will operate.

Disciplines to remember: A planet within three degrees of the cusp of a house of a higher number is said to be in the next house.

Award:

- Three points to the houses containing the luminaries
- Three points to the house containing Saturn
- Three points to the house containing the ruling planet
- Two points to houses containing planets in their own signs
- Two points to houses containing the accidental ruler of that house
- Two point to the house containing the natural ruler
- Three points for the house containing the north node
- Two points for the house containing the south node

- Two points for the house containing the part of fortune
- Two points to houses containing stationary planets
- Two points for houses containing stelliums
- Two points for houses containing the focal planets of yods and T-squares
- One point for each planet in a house, regardless of whether it has been counted in any of the above categories

Tally the points

Using the chart of Valentine.

House of ♀	1	2	3	4	5	6	7	8	9	10	11	12
☉		3									3	
☽						3						
♄				3								
ruling planet				3								
planet in own sign		2	2									
accidental ruler												
natural ruler		2	2									
☊								3				
♀♀		2										
⊗				2								
staty. planet												
stellium												
focal planets			2									
any planet		4	2	2		1						2
Total	0	13	8	10	0	4	0	3	1	1	3	2

Looking at the distribution according to the area of consciousness

Personal *Houses 1-4*	Relating *Houses 5-8*	Universal *Houses 9-12*
31	7	7

When considering the distribution between the twelve houses, equality is not to be expected, neither at the level of the individual houses nor at the level of areas of conscious.

- Indeed, if there is not a clear bias, then the scattered condition of the planets will be a factor of significance because it disperses energy and makes it difficult for a person to apply himself to any one task or undertaking.
- Another consideration if importance is whether the Sun, Moon, and Saturn occupy the same areas of consciousness or different areas.

☉	☽	♄
Personal	Relating	Personal

The analysis based upon house reveals the following:

- Valentine is focused upon the area of personal conscious (learning about self and how to project self), in particular upon the second house (values), the third house (communication), and the fourth house (self-understanding, awareness of past).
- The presence of Saturn in the same area of consciousness indicates that the psyche holds memory of this being an area of difficulty, with the fourth house being especially problematic.
- The Moon in the area of relating consciousness (the sixth house) indicates that service to others is a significant feature of the past life inheritance.

We will be referring to this prioritised information many times as we move on with the task of interpretation, but before we leave this section, we should summarise what it has told us so far:

Valentine's energy pattern is dominated by:

- The signs Aries and Aquarius
- The second house
- A square between Mercury and Pluto that will express itself through the third house where Mercury is its own house but in the sign of its fall.

This tells the esoterically oriented astrologer that in this lifetime, there is overriding need for Valentine to focus upon his own reality and to understand the power of conditioning and of the past, which are matters pertaining to the third and fourth houses. Mercury in Pisces is in its fall (i.e. the rational mind is waiting to fade out) to allow the intuition to become the guide, but before this can happen, he must first use his intellect to come to an understanding of himself, his circumstances, and the power of ideas to release himself from a habit of deferring to others.

The volatility and the lack of balance in this chart must be considered a liability.

We will examine the background to this in the next chapter.

Endnote

1. The precise definition of stationary is travelling at one tenth or less than its average daily motion. A planet is in stationary condition in the days immediately before it goes retrograde from direct or direct from retrograde. A computerised chart may not identify planets in this condition, whereas in an ephemeris, it is obvious. A stationary planet is very powerful and will dominate a chart. The number of aspects which it receives will determine how well it integrates with the other planets, and how well distributed is its energy. A poorly aspected stationary planet will operate in a compulsive way.

Chapter 15

Finding an Approach

When I began to work with astrology in the 1980s, Jungian psychology was the dominant influence upon contemporary British astrology. This approach was inspiring the majority of the new books being published in the astrology sector. I tried working with these concepts, but they simply did not interest me, which is not to say the standard of the work that the Jungians were doing was not good. Some (most) of it was excellent, but this approach did not supply the kind of insights that I had taken up astrology to find. So I set about devising my own approach, which is now enshrined in the DK Foundation's approach to horoscopical interpretation. Now, of course, there are students who do not find our approach interesting or rewarding, in which case we encourage them to find another kind of teaching. Where possible, we will make recommendations, because this is not a situation that should cause any embarrassment or offence. I am always glad when a student comes by this kind of awareness because it is a first step on the path to authenticity. Never stay with an approach that does not interest you: Life is too short and astrology too labour-intensive to make this advisable. If the way you are using astrology is not enabling you to get at information that excites and interests you, you have not yet found the approach that suits you. Keep on looking.

***

Astrology is a language we have to learn to use to make the natal chart, the map of the heavens, tell us what we wish to know.

The significance of this usually eludes the beginner, who has enough on getting to grips with basic technique. Eventually we discover that using astrology, we will only get answers to the questions we ask. An approach to interpretation is built through the quality and nature of the questions asked.

With reference to this point, please reread Chapter 1.

In this chapter, we are going to look at the four of the five key concepts that underpin the DK Foundation's approach to astrology, dealing with them in a very basic way (Endnote 1).

Here we are concerned with giving just enough information to make it possible to penetrate a natal chart and uncover useful information.

The four basic concepts are:

- Purpose
- Inheritance
- Creating the synthesis between past and present
- Creative contribution

The more knowledge we have about the luminaries, the planets, and the influence of the signs and houses, the better will be the quality of the information we have to hang upon the conceptual pegs.

Collecting this kind of information is something that an astrologer does throughout his or her life.

Working with the Key Concepts

Concept 1: Purpose

Underpinning question: *What am I here to do?*

The answer to this question is supplied by the Sun.

By sign and house position, the Sun describes the focus (house) and quality (sign) of the lifetime.

Developing this focus and quality of being is purposeful because it claims new ground for consciousness, by opening out new kinds of experiences, and restores balance. The reason for this may be evident from the position of the Moon and Saturn which, jointly, describe the inheritance.

Consider:

- The strength of the Sun . How many points does it score? (See Chapter Fourteen.)
- Planets that are in stressful aspect to the Sun will challenge efforts to move in the direction of the Sun .

Remember disciplines:

- Only planets that move slower than the Sun will have the power to frustrate.

- When the Sun is the stronger planet in a stressful aspect, the focus that it gives to the life will challenge the way that the faster planets are wanting to express themselves.

The context of the lifetime

The ascendant

The sign on the ascendant indicates the theme of a cycle of lives in which this lifetime takes its place. The ruling planet indicates the energy principle that the soul has made an issue during this cycle.

The north node

By sign and house position, the north node indicates the quality of consciousness to which experiences in this lifetime will add.

The part of fortune

By sign and house position, indicates the urge that drove the personality into incarnation.

Additional considerations:

Showing a child the way forward in life is considered to be a masculine function, and for this reason, in a natal chart, the Sun is a significator of the experience of the father in his capacity of director and inspirer:

- If the Sun is in stressful aspect to a significant number of planets, this is likely to indicate that the father performed this function through default (most commonly, this means he was absent) or by opposing the child.
- If just one or two planets are in major stressful aspect to the Sun, this indicates energies and areas of specific difficulty in the relationship with the father.
- These effects are reversed if the aspects with other planets are harmonious.

Concept 2: Inheritance

Under pinning question: What has formed the consciousness that I have brought into incarnation?

The answer to this question is supplied by the Moon and Saturn.

By sign and house position, the Moon describes the emotional constituent of the inheritance:

- The idea of self, formed in past life, that has come through into this lifetime.

- This idea is derived from the emotional reactions and indicates the kind of behaviour that we (unconsciously) assume will get us what we want.
- Our physical bodies are conditioned by this idea.

By sign and house position, Saturn indicates the mental constituent of the inheritance:

- The mindset that has been operative over lifetimes.
- The nature of the imbalance in consciousness that the present lifetime and cycle of lives is trying to correct.
- The cornerstone of the personal reality to which all new opportunities *I* directions will have to answer.

Consider:

- The strength of the Moon and Saturn as planets: How many points do they score? (see Chapter Fourteen).
- Planets that are in stressful aspect to the Moon and Saturn will challenge efforts to hold onto the past.
- The Moon and Saturn are natural allies, but they can be in stressful aspect to each other in a natal chart, in which case their friendship is suspended, unless the stressful contact is through a conjunction.

Remember disciplines:

- All planets in stressful aspect to the Moon, the fastest moving heavenly body, will challenge the inherited idea of self and this battle will be fought out on the emotional level.
- Only Chiron, Uranus, Neptune, and Pluto have the power to frustrate Saturn.
- When it is in stressful aspect to the inner planets, the Sun, and Jupiter, Saturn (representing the old mind set) will issue a major challenge. This is particularly significant when the challenge is to the Sun, the significator of the true identity.

The south node

By sign and house position, the south node indicates the quality of consciousness that is being left behind. Do the signs and house position of the Moon and Saturn reinforce this quality of consciousness is any direct and obvious way?

Additional considerations

Helping a person connect with the past is a feminine role. In a natal chart, the Moon represents the mother.

- If the Moon is in stressful aspect to a lot of planets, this indicates a difficult or denied relationship with the mother.
- If just one or two planets are in major stressful aspect to the Moon, this indicates energies and specific areas of difficulty in the relationship with the mother.
- These effects are reversed if the aspects with other planets are harmonious.

Saturn is the prime significator of the personality of the father (whereas the Sun describes the directing/inspiring function of the father)

- If Saturn is in stressful aspect to a lot of planets, this indicates a restricting and challenging father, or if Saturn is retrograde, a weak or absent father.
- If just one or two planets are in major stressful aspect to Saturn, then this indicates energies and specific areas of difficulty in the relationship with the father.
- These effects are reversed if the aspects with other planets are harmonious.
- Aspects between Saturn and the Moon always describe the experience of the mother rather than the father.

Concept 3: Creating the Synthesis

Underpinning question: How can the past be made to serve the present?

This question is answered by studying the relationship between the Sun, Moon, and Saturn.

Regardless of the ease or difficulty of this, the memory, qualities, and area of life described by the Moon have to be brought in line behind the qualities and area of life described by the Sun . Saturn has to be made to serve the Sun, not its natural ally, the Moon.

Consider:

- The nature of the experience conferred by the sign and house of the Sun (the present true identity) and that of the Moon (the ideas of self formed in past life). Are they compatible or the reverse? Regarding the aspect between the two luminaries: Is this stressful or harmonious, or is there no aspect between them at all? In the latter case, unless the two luminaries occupy the same sign, the two areas of life, represented by the two houses occupied by the luminaries, may operate without reference to each other.
- The above considerations need to be made with reference to each luminary and Saturn. Is Saturn in aspect to one or both luminaries, and if the latter, which is the stronger aspect? What is the nature of the aspect?
- How the mindset, disposition, and habits described by the sign and house position of Saturn can be made to serve the Sun?

Remember disciplines:

- The relative strength of the Sun and Moon will be enhanced by the number of planets they have on their side (harmonious aspects) and weakened by the number of challenges they receive (stressful aspects).
- Saturn will influence any faster planet with which it has contact.

Concept 4: Creative Contribution

Underpinning question: What is optimum use of my time and resources?

The question has to be asked in the context of the direction of a life and the focus provided by the Sun, and it is answerable chiefly by reference to the sign on the cusp of the fifth house, the house of creativity.

On the cusp of the fifth house	Nature of the creative energy
Aries	Life giving, lends itself to radiatory forms of healing, the martial arts
Taurus	Constructive, expresses itself through naturally occurring materials, particularly wood and clay
Gemini	Communicative, particularly adept with sound and words
Cancer	Nurturing, particularly concerned with children and child welfare, maternity, and other feminine issues
Leo	Performing, particularly drawn to dancing and acting
Virgo	Healing, whether of the physical vehicle or the soul
Libra	Harmonising, through music, design, or healing
Scorpio	Healing and illuminating through psychotherapeutic techniques or any means that shed light on the emotional patterns
Sagittarius	Teaching, particularly of life skills and spiritual values
Capricorn	Organising and entrepreneurial, particularly good in initiating roles
Aquarius	Strategising and speculative, often excels in mathematics, chess, and music
Pisces	Sacrificial, wishes to make available to others, both the personal resources and the fruits of the personal experience

Consider:

- The condition of the fifth house (i.e. the nature of any planets within it). Only Saturn has an inhibiting effect upon creativity. Uranus and Pluto confer exceptional creative capacity that may not want to express itself in a conventional way. The effect of Neptune is softer and less volatile.
- The inner planets incline toward a more conventional expression in accordance with the nature of the planet.
- The condition of the planet ruling the fifth house. If it receives challenging aspects from the outer planets, this will surely impede the creative flow.
- How the nature of the creative energy could best serve the purpose of the life as indicated by the placement of the Sun .

Additional considerations:

- The Sun in harmonious aspect to Uranus creates originality in whichever house the Sun is to be found in the natal chart. The conjunction aspect frequently confers genius.
- Mercury in stressful aspect to Uranus often results in dyslexia and learning difficulties, but in such cases, the intuitive powers are usually above average.
- The Moon in harmonious aspect to Neptune inclines a person toward the sublime that music and poetry are usually considered to express the best.

Applying these concepts to the chart of Valentine

(For the purposes of this exercise, we are using the Koch house system.)

In Chapter Fourteen, we examined Valentine's temperament.

Here we are going to look at his life by means of the four key concepts, knowing that whatever task it is that Valentine has to undertake, he will do it with volatility and passion.

Valentine's purpose: What is he here to do?

The Sun

When the Sun is in the second house, it is evidence of a lifetime in which the requirement is to establish the value system and live in accordance with it. In the second house, a person externalises and organises himself around what he desires.

The second house is one of the houses of personal consciousness (i.e. where a person is required to find out about himself).

It brings experiences that encourage a person to find out what is important to him personally and what he truly desires. His experiences in this house may require him to challenge social values and it is a mistake to think, as so many astrology students do, that this house confers a cautious, materialistic perspective. That will depend entirely upon the sign on the cusp of the second and the planets within it.

Valentine has Capricorn on the cusp of the second house, which is materialistic, and he has Venus in Capricorn close the cusp and working in the second house, which confers a love of possessions, but in the house is an intercepted sign, Aquarius containing the Sun, Uranus, and Neptune.

Interceptions are considered to be evidence of latency (i.e. the Aquarian influence will come to take over from that of Capricorn as his life unfolds), bringing with it a more inventive approach to acquisition and spending that will be inspired, not by the Capricornian concern with security, but by the Aquarian desire for freedom.

If we look at the worksheets made out for Valentine, we will see that the number of points scored by the sign Aquarius makes it is a much stronger influence in his make-up than that of Capricorn.

Counting the number of points scored by the second house itself, we find it to record the highest of all the twelve houses. This will mean that the second house, and those things governed by it will exert a powerful influence upon Valentine's consciousness.

Only an aspect from Saturn to the Sun, or from Pluto to Uranus or Neptune, could effectively deflect the energy going through the second house planets. But, in fact, the contacts from those planets are out of orbs.

The conjunction in the second house of Uranus and the Sun will confer a remarkable inventiveness in second house matters, but this will be at the expense of structures and formality. Both Uranus and Neptune are banishing principles and Neptune, when in the second house, inclines toward fantasising and grandiose schemes

Summary:

Valentine is here to uncover his individuality through his dealings with the things that matter to him: money and freedom.

The context of the lifetime

The ascendant

With Sagittarius on the ascendant, Jupiter is the orthodox ruling planet and Earth the esoteric ruler.

Jupiter is in Aries in the fourth house. Earth, which is always to be found directly opposite the Sun, is in Leo in the eighth house.

The message here is that this is a cycle the theme of which is the integration of higher and lower (Sagittarius) and specifically integration of desire (the eighth house) and the past (the fourth hosue).

This lifetime with its emphasis on money and values is a part of this larger process.

The north node

The north node is in Leo in the eighth house indicating that Valentine is moving towards a greater awareness of other people and, eventually, into compassion.

It is to be noted that the Sun is to be found in the house of the south node, indicating that this life with its focus upon money and personal values represents a strategy to shake consciousness free from personal desires and yearning by a means, best described as letting him get it out of his system.

When we study a lot of charts, we will begin to recognise the strategies of the soul.

The part of fortune

The part of fortune is near the cusp of the fourth house (IC) and operating in that house, indicating that the drive into incarnation was provided by the need to make his peace with the feminine principle, expressed through the mother, the past, and his own psyche. In this lifetime, he is being invited to explore an aspect of his psyche (i.e. his desire nature through externalising it).

Valentine's Inheritance: What has formed the consciousness he has brought into incarnation

The Moon

In the sixth house, the Moon describes an idea of self based upon being of service to others. In the sign Gemini, this indicates an intellectual decision to follow such a lifestyle.

Experiences in the sixth house involve the subordinating of the will and personal desires to the needs of others and to hard work.

In this memory may be found the explanation for the weight of the emphasis upon exploring personal desire in the present incarnation. This kind of experience is required to re-establish balance.

On examining the worksheets, we find that the Moon is a significantly stronger planet than the Sun, and this will means that the pull from the Moon back into a service mentality will be powerful (especially when young when the influence of the Moon is at its height). But the Moon is opposed by Pluto, the most powerful planet in the chart and the ruler of the eleventh house. This indicates that the social code of the times into which Valentine has been born challenge the memory of servitude, which will weaken the influence of the Moon as time goes by. Moreover, the sixth house is not as powerful a channel for planetary energy as the second house, meriting a score of only four against an eleven for the second house.

It should be noted, however, that the Moon is in trine aspect to the Sun, which indicates that to some degree, the past life memory is able to assist the establishment of the new direction in this lifetime, most obviously through the willingness to work hard and earn money.

Saturn

Saturn in the fifth house indicates difficulty in expressing and believing in one's worth as an individual. It is frequently the product of religious conditioning, which emphasises sin and human baseness. The influence of Taurus suggests that a preoccupation with the practicalities of life created awareness of the concept of self-indulgence. The fear of being self-indulgent has been a major cause of inhibition.

Saturn in the fifth house almost always indicates a stern and repressive father.

Esotericism considers that Saturn is older than the Moon, and this self-doubting, self-flagellating perspective is the cornerstone of Valentine's consciousness.

Saturn is not an exceptionally powerful planet in Valentine's chart, although it is significantly stronger than the Sun. But it makes no aspect to the Sun (except the contraparallel with which we are not concerned at this level). The semi-sextile that it makes with the Moon is not a major aspect, but it is enough to create conversance between the two levels of memory and reinforce the hardworking, materialistic ethic. Jupiter, also in the fourth hosue (and evidence of a liberal, spirited mother), cannot much help because it is dominated by Saturn, but Neptune and Uranus will use the square aspect between them and Saturn to challenge its rigidity in a subversive and sporadic way.

We must conclude from this that Valentine will start his lifetime in the grip of the Protestant work ethic, but will become attracted to less labour-intensive ways of becoming prosperous to have more freedom and release himself from a punitive working regime.

The tension between the second house with its Aquarian influence and the fifth house, which is dominated by self-doubting Saturn in Taurus, will be severe indeed. Valentine will experience himself as inhibited: a visionary who finds it difficult to believe in the value his own visions and his ability to realise them.

In a life, such conflicts will be the source of much suffering until we deal with them.

The south node

The south node in the second house in Aquarius indicates that consciousness has been formed by ideas about material matters held by the collectivity or society and that he has yet to become receptive to individual desires and more humane values (Leo, sign of north node).

The inheritance, therefore, is of a cautious, hardworking approach to material security. Valentine appears to have met the memory externalised in the personality of his father.

Creating the synthesis: How Valentine will make the past serve the present

As noted previously, Valentine's Moon is in trine aspect to the Sun, which will assist the task of integrating the idea of self developed on past life with the requirements of this life. The willingness to work hard and the receptivity to ideas (both the Sun and the Moon are in air signs) will help him adapt the inherited idea of self to the requirements of his rightful identity. All syntheses must be Sun-led.

More challenging, however, is the Saturnian memory, which represents the cornerstone of Valentine's reality and will conspire to keep him in a state of underachievement, when the requirement of this lifetime is to go for it.

If this Saturnian memory is not to sabotage him by joining forces with the Moon and persuading him to play safe, he will need to become conscious of it (and this is one of the benefits of an astrological reading) and learn how to push through self-doubt and self-questioning when it starts, as it surely will when he considers any new undertaking.

The danger of a chart like this that confers such a volatile temperament is that he will shy away from undertaking anything of significance because of the fear of failure or even the fear of being presumptuous (Who am I to do that? is a common question from a person with Saturn in fifth house) and squander his energy in activities that bring excitement and release but amount to nothing.

The other danger is what the old astrology books would describe somewhat sternly as a lack of measure. Mental impetuosity is a feature of Sun-conjunct Uranus. If he does not get the balance right and, under the influence of Saturn and the Moon, this makes playing safe his default setting. Certainly, he will break out into recklessness through boredom and the need to escape the drudgery of hard work and routine. In these circumstances, his energy flow will be erratic, swinging from conformity to rebellion and back to conformity via a sense of shame or contrition.

This kind of erratic behaviour is frequently the product of absence of synthesis between past and present, and is a waste of both time and energy.

Planets that make harmonious contact to both the Sun and Saturn or the Sun and the Moon can be of help in steadying the energy flow.

In Valentine's case, the only real contender is Jupiter in the fourth house, which is sextile the Sun and conjunct Saturn. Although Jupiter is weakened by this contact with Saturn, it is still able to assist the Sun to some degree and indicates that an interest in self-understanding (encouraged by his mother) could help him with this problem of erratic behaviour.

Creating the synthesis takes time; in most cases, it takes a substantial portion of our adult life.

Creative contribution: What will be the optimum use of Valentine's time and resources

We know that Valentine's interest is in money and using his resources in a way that enhances his freedom. His chosen field of work is likely to be some aspect of financial services, starting probably in accountancy and banking, which is safe, and then, perhaps, moving into something more speculative.

With Taurus on the cusp of the fifth house, he is unlikely to move too far away from the physical presence of money. He will like to see it, handle it and be around it.

Venus, the ruling planet of Taurus and the significator of his creativity is in the second house in Capricorn, which indicates that the optimum use of his resources is going to be structuring financial systems.

Valentine, with his Uranian personality, may prove to be one of the architects of a new financial order that operates according to the laws of the soul, of which Uranus is the agent, not the acquisitive, exclusive ways of the personality. But whether this becomes the case for Valentine will depend upon whether such things are of interest to him. One thing we know for sure about this life is that it is a given to him to live in accordance with his own values.

It will be the extent of his interest in nonpersonal goals that will determine the quality of his contribution. The potential to have such a perspective is present but, in the final analysis, it is the awareness that is developed by his experience that will decide this.

The astrologer's role is to identify the potential, define the challenges, recognise the opportunity, and explain the purpose of a life. After this, it is a matter between a person and Providence.

Conclusion

These four concepts provide a basic approach to Valentine's life that can then be enhanced with detail.

The effect of the aspect configurations needs to be considered, for example. The T-square that has Mercury as it focal planet has the ninth house (overseas travel *I* questing) as its empty quarter. Does this indicate that Valentine will resolve the tensions in life better overseas? This is a matter for consideration.

Be led by client questions. This may sound daunting, but, it is common sense. What is the point of overloading a reading with unsolicited detail that may not be of interest to the client? If, as the astrologer, we offer what we consider to be of fundamental importance to the understanding of the life, we can then let the reading find its own level.

Remember that it is quality of information, not its quantity, that makes a good reading.

Endnote

1. We look at these four concepts in more detail in *Transitional Astrology,* where they are put into a cosmic context. The fifth concept, opportunity, requires a knowledge of time-working techniques, which are the concern of the book *Working with Time.*

Chapter 16

Making it Meaningful

Obviously, accuracy and a sound grasp of astrological principles help make a good astrologer, but if we intend to share our knowledge with others, whether professionally or vocationally, that is only a part of the requirement. The other qualifications are an interest, liking, and respect for people and their individual opportunities and a genuine desire to communicate a way of understanding that we truly believe will be helpful to another. This does not necessitate a great store of esoteric knowledge, but it does require firsthand experience of the ongoing task of consciously trying to sort out one's own life through a process of challenging oneself and one's patterns. Only then will we appreciate how hard it is to fight free of conditioning to be more authentic and more truly ourselves. Of their nature, astrological readings are prescriptive, and if they are to avoid tipping over into judgment or preaching, a willingness to share is essential. This does not mean swapping experiences; it means sharing our humanity. One cannot learn humanity theoretically; we come by it through experience of life.

✳✳✳

The Golden Rules

Every astrologer has to find his or her own level. To be convincing to others, one has to believe in what one is saying and in the effectiveness of the approach. There are a few golden rules that cannot be broken if one would inspire trust in others.

Rule 1. Avoid using concepts that may be fashionable, but in which one has no faith or interest. Offer the kind of approach you yourself would find useful.

Rule 2. Do not try to be all things to all people. Build upon the aim of being helpful to those with whom you are able to share. The law of attraction will do the rest. It is only on the physical level that opposites attract: Like attracts like, emotionally and spiritually.

Rule 3. The function of an astrologer is to inform, not to please, reassure, entertain, or fix.

Rule 4. Never say things that you do not mean, and be aware of the borderline that separates tact from dishonesty. If you are expressing an opinion as distinct from making an assessment from the chart, say so.

Rule 5. If you find you do not enjoy sharing your astrological knowledge with others, quit! If you do, give it 100%, and it will give you back 200%.

Setting your own questions

In support of finding a meaningful approach to astrology, students are encouraged to list questions they consider important because finding answers to these questions would help them understand their own lives better. Those questions will provide pegs upon which much useful knowledge can be hung. This is a far more effective way of getting into interpretation than trying to memorise a lot of information that may or may not be useful to you.

Reproduced below are the ten questions of a former DK Foundations student and the replies given to help her organise her thinking in this area and develop suitable expectations.

1. What is the purpose of this lifetime, in terms of individual transformation and the collective good?

The purpose of any lifetime, whether human or animal, is the transformation of energy. As we move off the energy of the Moon and into the energy of the Sun, as defined by its sign and house placement, we transform energy. This movement is transformative, per se, and is not dependent upon certain signs being more advanced than others.

Indeed, this idea of there being a hierarchy among the signs and houses is an irrelevance in horoscopy and needs to be eradicated. There are astrologers who find it impossible to conceive that a person with the Sun in an earth house and an earth sign could be more advanced than a Pisces working through the twelfth house. This is because they have no appreciation of the process of development and are caught up in astrological cliches, among which is a tendency, to equate mystical capacity (Pisces/the twelfth house) with an advanced level of spirituality. It is nothing of the sort: Mystical capacity is functional in that it opens certain development opportunities; it is not, of itself, a measure of development.

So, moving from the Moon to the Sun is transformative of itself, whatever the signs and houses involved. This is because to honour the requirement of the Sun sign involves a degree of consciousness that is relatively higher than that required to express the energy of the Moon, which (with Saturn) is the assemblage point of memory and unconscious patterns.

When a person has no concept of progress or an awareness of what is truly involved in personal development (i.e. sacrifice and struggle), then the chances are that the life will reassemble itself around the Moon.

The ascendant provides continuity of a supervisory kind, being the point of interface between the personality and its informing life, the soul. Eventually, the energy of the ascendant, the ruler of the ascendant, and the Sun sign have to be synthesised, but it is the Sun, by sign and house placement, that defines the purpose and the direction of the life.

A person who is transforming energy in accordance with the blue print of his life, ipso facto, is doing his bit for the collectivity that is humanity. Esotericism recognises that expressing themselves through humanity are seven soul groupings, each with a specific kind of job to do. The seven groups express themselves through the twelve Sun signs.

2.   What should I be doing? What am I here to do?

We are here to transform energy and learn through relationship, along the lines indicated by the natal chart. This is our basic purpose.

To use the signs and house placements will enable us to understand what this transformation means in terms of a shift in consciousness.

To explore what is involved, practically speaking, in giving expression to the energy of the Sun, by sign and house placement, will bring purpose down to an everyday level. A popular astrology book (Linda Goodman's *Sun Signs* is particularly good) may be useful tool for coming to grips with the practical ways in which the Sun expresses itself through the signs and the houses.

Also to be taken into consideration is the sign and house placement of the ruler of the Sun sign, Mars, and the ruler of the ascendant. These planets provide additional information about the way the energy is trying express itself. The assumption is that cooperation with the blueprint will enable a person to give optimum expression of the energy of the personality.

Bear in mind that a person is likely to feel far more familiar and therefore more comfortable about expressing the Moon's placement and may be quite resistant to the area of life indicated by the Sun.

3.   To what should I be committed?

We all need to be committed to progress if we want to make maximum use of the opportunities provided with our lifetimes

This involves thoroughly understanding what progress means in the context of our life:

- In terms of a shift in consciousness
- In terms of how to give it practical expression in everyday life and practical expression of our purpose

• In terms of acceptance and appreciation of the struggle and sacrifice required to keep ourselves moving forward

4. What past life influences are acting on me in this lifetime?

The Moon and Saturn provide continuity, but unlike the ascendant, which also provides continuity, the continuity of the Moon and Saturn is the product of the process of evolution. It is the what is/ what has been achieved aspect of development, as distinct from the what is to be. It is the reality of the matter, as distinct from the plan, of which the ascendant holds the secret.

To examine the Moon by sign and house placement is to uncover the idea *I* image of self that dominates the psyche.

To examine Saturn by house placement is to identify the mindset that has been building over lifetimes through many personality forms. Saturn is much older than the Moon.

The aspect between the Moon and Saturn will indicate the extent to which the recent idea of self challenged or reinforced the mindset.

5. In which areas of my life are habitual patterns holding me back and in need of transformation?

The Moon and Saturn are the two significators of the past. In both cases, consider also the planets disposited by the Moon and Saturn because the two dispositors show the energy (planet) and the area of life (house) by which and into which the past life memory is carried. Join these points, and you have what is called the Moon complex.

This complex comprises energies in which memory resonates and that will set up a undertow and pull the unwary person back into the past. We examine this idea more thoroughly in *Transitional Astrology.*

6. What skills and talents do I possess that would benefit from cultivation?

When the Sun's position has been carefully examined, and also that of the ruler of the Sun sign (ie. the planet disposited by the Sun), as well as the ruler of the ascendant, in order to ascertain the kind of activities to which the creative capacities should be directed, look at the sign on the cusp of the fifth house and ascertain the position of the ruler of this sign. This will describe the quality (sign) of the creative force and the area of life (house occupied by the ruler of this sign) through which this energy will want to work.

Consider also the capacities that have been developed in the past (by means of the harmonious aspects thrown by the Moon to other planets). Provided that these energies are redirected, so that they serve the theme that the Sun, rather than the Moon brings into the life, this is an economical use of the resources.

7.   Am I meant to have children / be a parent?

Like that that of relationship, this tends to be an area of life in which we hope we can avoid the need to think intelligently. We want the issue to be emotive and abstruse, in order, perhaps, to put it beyond the responsibility of making a conscious decision until we have suffered enough that is.

Parenthood involves a certain use of the time and energy, it can produce a certain kind of return, but only a certain kind, and strongly individual people need to work out for themselves, the best that they can, whether the return is going to be adequate compensation for the sacrifices. This is a basic act of responsibility.

Decisions about whether to have children are spiritually significant only in as much the having them, or not having them, will create certain conditions in the life that a person will then have to perform against.

The natal chart will give indications of the likelihood of the return being considered to exceed the payment due. These include:

- The Sun, inner planets, and Jupiter in the sign or house of Cancer or in harmonious aspect with the ruler of the fourth house
- The Sun, inner planets, and Jupiter in the sign, but not the house, of Leo
- Venus and Jupiter (and to a lesser extent, the Sun, Mercury, and Mars) in the eleventh house or in harmonious aspect with the ruler of the eleventh house
- The Moon conjunct, sextile, or trine of Venus or Jupiter
- The Moon in Cancer will create a strong instinctive urge to have children, but whether this course of action will fit comfortably with the developmental requirement of the lifetime will have to be examined
- When the Moon conjunct or square Saturn or Saturn is in the fourth house, parenting is perceived to be a material and emotional struggle.

The indications that parenthood may prove onerous and restricting include:

- Uranus in the sign Cancer
- Uranus in the sign Leo
- Saturn in eleventh house
- Uranus in eleventh house

8.   What qualities do I need to develop to become whole and integrated?

Social conditioning is the biggest enemy of authenticity. If we define a person's purpose carefully and then present it to that person, from the reaction to what, after all, is a description of the true identity, we can find out what are the areas of inhibition that stand to frustrate the outworking of the plan of the life. The place of Saturn is an obvious area of restriction in the psyche, but there may be others.

For example, the planets Uranus and Pluto, and in a more subtle way Neptune, are all banishing principles: They banish the personality from those areas of life; to cooperate with this requirement spares a lot of pain. Is the individual aware that this is the case, or is he hanging on, trying to wring out of these areas of life the fulfillment that is eluding him or her?

If the Sun is there with the banishing principles, there is a need to give a fully conscious expression in this area of the chart. This combination of the Sun in conjunction with the banishing principles frequently results in an exceptional expression because it enables a person to transcend the limitations of personality consciousness and conditioned expression.

9.   Why are intimate relationships difficult for me? What do I need to learn to have more successful ones?

Our relationship experiences are contained within the design for our lives; they do not come from outside it, nor are they protected from our personality patterns.

Think about this. We are inclined to think that a stable, loving relationship is a right when it is nothing of the kind. Our personal relationships are the prime learning tool, and our experiences in them will reflect our realities. In many cases, our close relationships bear the brunt of our learning.

- Examine the seventh house to find out what the chart has to say about relationships specifically.
- Examine the sign and condition of Venus to discover to what we are attracted. If, for example, it is freedom (Sagittarius/Aquarius), consider the implications of this for a conventional relationship.
- Examine the condition of the Moon to uncover the emotional track record and the predisposition. The Moon in Libra or the seventh house may predispose a person toward an early marriage, but eventually, this will have to be synthesised with the developmental requirement of the present lifetime.
- Assess how commitment will fit into the design for the life. If it cannot support a
- conventional commitment than another kind of association should be encouraged.
- Find out what fits the design of the life, and assess expectation against this.

Remember that it is not situations themselves that cause suffering, but our expectation that things should be other than they are.

10. How can I be of service?

Firstly, it is important to be clear about what service is. Service is an approach to working; it is motivation, rather than a specific kind of work. A focus upon the form of work tends to encourage a priggish attitude that identifies certain jobs as being spiritually correct, and others, usually those that are essential to the running of a modern society, of which we are all a part, as worthless. The result is a withholding of both capacity and respect.

Master DK has given the following definition of service: Service is recognising a need and knowing how to go about meeting it.

We all serve from where we stand, with whatever capacities the chart shows us to have. When we can free ourselves from selfish motivation and offer our best, through whatever frame is available to us at any one time, in a spirit of cooperation and purposefulness, then that is service.

> **If you have found this approach helpful, there is a wide range of articles on astrology and esoteric matters, frequently updated and freely available, on the DK Foundation website: www.dkfoundation.co.uk.**

About the Author

Suzanne Rough is a philosophy graduate and has been a practicing astrologer and teacher since 1989. Between 1994 and 2006, she was tutored by Master Djwal Khul (DK), and in 1998, she established the DK Foundation School of Astrology to share his insights and encourage the next generation of astrology practitioners.

About the Book

The aim of this book is to introduce students of astrology to an approach that will make horoscopy's conventional techniques useful to those who approach astrology hoping for spiritual guidance. This is not about learning a new astrological language, but rather how to give a different application to the familiar techniques of Western horoscopy.

Understanding the Natal Chart is recommended to complete beginners, those wishing to structure patchy knowledge, and those already competent in horoscopy who are in search of a more esoteric approach to see the way forward.